HILL COUNTRY

C H R O N I C L E S

HILL COUNTRY

CHRONICLES

CLAY COPPEDGE

Charleston   London

THE
History
PRESS

Published by The History Press
Charleston, SC 29403
www.historypress.net

Cover image: Blanco County Courthouse. *Courtesy of the Texas State Library.*

First published 2010
Second printing 2011
Third printing 2011

Manufactured in the United States

ISBN 978.1.59629.980.1

Coppedge, Clay.
Hill Country chronicles / Clay Coppedge.
p. cm.
Includes bibliographical references.
ISBN 978-1-59629-980-1
1. Texas Hill Country (Tex.)--History. 2. Texas Hill Country (Tex.)--History, Local. 3.
Texas Hill Country (Tex.)--Biography. 4. Texas Hill Country (Tex.)--Social life and customs.
I. Title.
F392.T47C67 2010
976.4'31--dc22
2010024441

*Dedicated to the memories of A.C. Greene, Jim Bowmer
and Bob and Nancy Coppedge.*

CONTENTS

PREFACE

Most of these stories first appeared, sometimes in different form, in the *Country World* newspaper, a division of Echo Publishing, Inc. "In Praise of the Unappreciated Mule," "Camels for Texas," "Cowboy King of Polo," "Plight of the Pleurocoeleus," "Thanksgiving as a Texas Thang," "Charcoal Burners and Cedar Choppers" and "The Reindeer of Texas" first appeared in *Texas Co-op Power* magazine.

Part I

A FORBIDDING LAND

EASTER FIRES

In the wake of the French Revolution of the 1830s, German princes ruled their provinces with what can charitably be called an iron hand, forcing thousands of students, professors, craftsmen and farmers out of the country. Some of those dispossessed Germans looked toward Texas as a true "land of the free," a place to start over. Glowing descriptions of the state in travel books and brochures were, unfortunately for the immigrants, more poetic than accurate.

The group that probably suffered the most from the Texas propaganda was the Mainzer Adelsverein, a group of noblemen led by Baron Otfriend Hans Freiherr von Meusebach. He Americanized his name to "John Meusebach" on the boat from Germany. The Comanches would know him as "El Sol Colorado" because of his flowing red beard.

Once in Texas, the Adelsverein suffered a shortage of wagons to transport them from the coast, where people were having considerable difficulties with Mexico. They were also short on money but carried a surplus of debt and disease as they made their way to the three million acres of the Fisher-Miller land grant, of which the Comanches knew nothing.

Meusebach bought ten thousand acres of wilderness land near the Pedernales River on credit and, with about 120 of his fellow immigrants,

John O. Meusebach negotiated a treaty that kept Fredericksburg relatively free of the Comanche raids that plagued the rest of the Hill Country.

built an outpost called Fredericksburg in honor of Prince Frederick of Prussia, who helped finance the Adelsverein. Survivors of the trek and the settlement's early days began the work of moving from tents into actual structures, planting crops and forming militias to protect against Indian attacks. A year later, more than five hundred German immigrants were living in the new outpost.

Meusebach knew he had to deal with the Comanches if the Adelsverein was to settle any of the expansive land grant. Conventional wisdom held that meeting with the Comanches, peacefully or not, was a form of suicide. The tribe's depredations in the Hill Country were many and gruesome. The community of Baby Head supposedly got its name because the Comanches left a baby's head, impaled on a spike or fence post, as a message to other would-be settlers.

Somehow, Meusebach, speaking through Indian interpreter Jim Shaw, was able to reach an accord with the Comanche. He negotiated with Comanche chiefs Buffalo Hump, Santa Anna, Old Owl and others at the San Saba River, not far from Mason, in March 1847. Meusebach offered the Comanches some $3,000 worth of presents in exchange for not harming the surveyors or settlers he aimed to turn loose in the territory. Surveyors were special targets of the Indians, who believed that the surveying equipment was what allowed the white settlers to steal their land, which was true, but in a way that the Comanches would have seen as hopelessly abstract.

The treaty stated in part: "In regard to the settlements on the Llano the Comanches promise not to disturb or in any way molest the German colonists, on the contrary to assist them, also to give notice if they see bad Indians about the settlement who come to steal horses from or in any way molest the Germans—the Germans likewise promising to aid the Comanches against their enemies, should they be in danger of having their horses stolen or in any way to be injured. And both parties agree, that if there be any difficulties or any wrong done by single bad men, to bring the same before the chiefs to be finally settled and decided by the agent of our great father." The deal was sealed in Fredericksburg on May 9, 1847, when the Comanche chiefs came to town to accept their gifts.

The treaty was a turning point for the settlement and one of the most noteworthy contributions of many that German immigrants made to Texas, but the days leading up to the final negotiations on the San Saba were tense. Comanches lurked every which way in the hills as Meusebach and the Germans made their way north. It was an unsettled time and people were on edge.

Supposedly, the Comanches lit signal fires along the hilltops to let the chiefs know where the Germans were and how many men were traveling to the San Saba. Other accounts describe the fires as simply campfires. Either way, the fires lit up the night and terrified some small children in an unprotected Fredericksburg cabin. The children asked their mother why the fires were burning. Were the Comanches coming? Were they going to die? The mother reassured the children by telling them that the fires would heat great cauldrons in which Easter eggs would be boiled and that the eggs would be painted with dye from wildflowers that other rabbits had gathered in anticipation of the Easter rabbit's arrival. The children went to sleep feeling safe and protected. Peace soon descended upon the land.

That's the story of the Easter Fires, a foundation of the legend and lore of Fredericksburg's founding. For a while, it was told that the tradition of the Easter Fires actually started in Fredericksburg, but the tradition of the

Easter Fires can actually be traced all the way back to pre-Christian times as a pagan ritual of spring, one that was incorporated by Teutonic Christianity.

Germans had been lighting Easter Fires on the Saturday evening preceding Easter for centuries before anybody in Europe had ever heard of the New World or Texas. Meusebach met with the Comanches on March 1 and 2, but Easter fell on April 3 that year, which brings us back to that house in which the mother tried to soothe her children's fears. Since Easter Fires weren't lit in every German province, the mother might have been from an area that didn't observe the ritual, or maybe she told them that it was going to take a month to get the eggs ready. Who knows?

Maybe the stories of Meusebach's pilgrimage of peace and the lighting of the fires simply merged in the public mind to form one good story, one that serves as a snapshot of those uneasy times. Even if it didn't happen just the way it is told, it should have.

THE SCALPING OF JOSIAH WILBARGER

After 180 years, the Josiah Wilbarger story still contains for a lot of people elements of fact and fantasy, but some of us prefer to swallow the whole story—hook, line and legend. Since few of us have ever survived a scalping, the inclination here is to believe the words of one who did.

Josiah Wilbarger was originally from Missouri. He left that state about 1827 and was one of the earliest settlers of the Stephen F. Austin colony. After stints in Matagorda and La Grange, he built a plantation and sawmill on the Colorado River about ten miles from Bastrop. Fertile land, fish, game and lumber were abundant—but so were Indians.

He had a fateful encounter with either Comanches or Apaches in 1830 as he surveyed the north bank of the Colorado River between Bastrop and Austin. There he joined up with four other men to scout some land in Reuben Hornsby's land grant when they spied an Indian and gave chase but lost him. Stopping for lunch at the Pecan Springs area of present-day Austin, three of the men unsaddled and hobbled their horses, while the other two left their horses saddled and staked during the break. That turned out to be a crucial decision. When the attack came, the men who had left their horses saddled were able to escape on horseback; the other three were left to fend for themselves, and that did not go well.

Josiah Wilbarger was scalped and lived to tell that tale—along with a remarkable twist. *Texas State Library.*

The two men with Wilbarger were killed, and the warriors had every reason to believe that they had killed Wilbarger, too. The arrows in either leg didn't appear fatal, but the rifle ball he took to the back of the neck certainly did. The shot paralyzed him but left him alive and conscious. He was fully aware of his scalp being lifted, but he experienced nothing other than a sound "like distant thunder" while it was happening.

Later, when he was able to move again, he also was able to feel pain. He tried to crawl away in the general direction of Hornsby's place but only made it a few hundred yards to a large oak tree, where he fell into a deep sleep and dreamed that he saw his sister, Margaret. She encouraged him and told him not to move from that spot because help would soon be on the way. Though he had no way of knowing it at the time, his sister had died the previous day. Wilbarger last saw her drifting away in his dream toward the Hornsby place.

The next two dreams belonged to Sally Hornsby, Reuben's wife. After hearing the story of the attack from the survivors, she went to bed and dreamed that she saw Wilbarger lying under a tree, badly wounded but alive. She woke up from the first dream, told her husband about it, went back to sleep and had the same dream again. There was no going back to sleep after that. At her insistence, a search party ventured back to the scene of the attack and found Wilbarger under the oak tree. The first man to see him thought that he was an Indian and was about to shoot when Wilbarger managed to call out, "Don't shoot! It's Wilbarger."

Josiah Wilbarger recovered at Hornsby's place but not fully. He lived another eleven years, but the wound was a constant source of worry and pain for him, causing him to wear a silk stocking over an area that remained exposed. His doctor suspected that Wilbarger's death was hastened by the old injury after he banged his head on a low doorway of his home and never recovered.

J.W. Wilbarger, Josiah's brother, wrote and compiled the book *Indian Depredations in Texas*, which was first published in 1889 when many of the depredations were closer to current events than history. He recounted the attack in sometimes grisly detail and commented on the series of dreams that saved his brother's life. "We leave to those more learned the task of explaining the strange coincidence of the visions of Wilbarger and Mrs. Hornsby," J.W. Wilbarger wrote. "It must remain a marvel and a mystery."

The scalping of his brother and killing of the two men with him, believed to be the first such bloodshed in Travis County, is one of several hundred such stories recounted in Wilbarger's book. Aside from its value to the state's history, it's also enlightening to browse for anyone who thinks that settling the state in the 1830s was a whole lot of fun.

PACKSADDLE MOUNTAIN

As mountains go, Packsaddle Mountain isn't a lot to look at, even though it can be exceedingly beautiful in certain lights. It's about 1,600 feet at its highest point and would hardly be described as majestic. Located about five miles east of Kingsland in eastern Llano County, Packsaddle Mountain makes up in legend and lore what it might lack in grandeur, though much of the legend and lore is contradictory.

Even the origin of its name is in dispute. Was it named because its twin peaks look like a packsaddle, or did early settlers find a packsaddle there and named the mountain for that? Accounts differ. What's the real story about the mine that was supposedly there? Was it Jim Bowie's silver mine? Did the Spanish work it until they were attacked by Indians, or was it the Indians' mine until the Spanish attacked them? Again, accounts differ.

One story has it that the Los Almagres gold and silver mine was located atop Packsaddle Mountain after Don Bernardo de Mirango found a rich vein in 1757. The mine was worked for the better part of two decades until a large group of Indians attacked. Realizing that they were about to be killed, the miners filled in the mine so the Indians wouldn't have access to it. Or maybe the Indians worked the mines until the Spanish launched an unsuccessful assault—the Spanish attackers were all killed in the process, and the Indians, fearing a larger and more successful assault from a Spanish settlement at present-day Menard on the San Saba River, filled in the mine and landscaped the area to make it indistinguishable from the rest of the mountain. Either way, we know that something violent happened there because the top of the mountain was littered with human bones for many years afterwards.

Packsaddle Mountain was the site of more violence in August 1873. A group of hostiles, most likely Apaches, set up camp on top of the mountain and used it as a launching point for attacks on ranches in the

Packsaddle Mountain was the scene of the last Indian battle in Llano County.

valley below. The Moss Ranch was one of those ranches. When one of the ranch's cows showed up with an arrow in its side, eight men rode from the ranch in search of the original owner of that particular arrow. On their way up Packsaddle Mountain, they saw an Indian and gave chase, which led to them to a group of twenty or so other Indians who were busy processing a cow that hadn't made it back to Moss's ranch.

Armed as they were with Colt six-shooters and Spencer carbines—the the automatic rifles of their day—the cowboys liked their odds enough to attack, but the battle did not get off to a good start for the cowboys; four were wounded during a mad dash aimed at cutting the Apaches off from their horses. The Apaches then mounted a series of charges in an attempt to recover their horses but were repelled each time by a withering blanket of rifle fire. When the Indians regrouped behind some brush, out of sight, the cowboys began attending to their wounded. The warriors used that opportunity to mount another attack but were again forced back.

At this point in the battle, a young chief, who was obviously long on courage but perhaps short on judgment, urged his warriors to attack again, but his warriors held back, reluctant to face again the relentless barrage of bullets. Maybe to show his braves what an easy thing he was asking of them, or as an act of suicide, the chief began a solo advance on the cowboys, pausing every few feet to fire a Winchester in their direction. When he came into range of the Spencers, the men from the Moss Ranch opened fire, and the chief fell dead.

The remaining Apaches left the chief and two other dead warriors where they had fallen and departed Packsaddle Mountain without their horses, weapons, blankets, saddle or anything else other than their lives. Rather than give chase to the Indians, the Moss Ranch cowboys tended to their wounded, all of whom recovered, and gathered the spoils of battle. It was the last Indian battle in Llano County but not the last time that Packsaddle Mountain was a location of interest.

In 1924, two men from Austin claimed to have found the old mine of Packsaddle Mountain legend and lore and proclaimed that Texas was about to become the richest mining state in the country. It never happened, just as numerous other attempts to locate the mine over the years came to nothing. While it's easy to understand the disappointment of people who invested money and part of their lives in locating the mine, the rest of us can be glad that no one ever found the mine. No one who has ever seen Packsaddle Mountain in daylight's first or twilight's last gleaming is likely to either forget it or describe it in a way that does it justice. In today's world, that's a real treasure.

Trail of the Tonkawas

At certain places on certain rivers in Texas you can see trees bent in the direction of the water. The trees weren't bent by the wind over centuries but rather by Tonkawa Indians, who lived along those rivers long before the arrival of settlers. The land stretching from atop the Edwards Plateau south to the coastal plains and east and northeast to the Brazos River Bottoms was the heart of Tonkawa territory. Sugar Loaf Mountain in Milam County is identified by some Tonkawas as the place where the tribe originated, when a wolf sniffed them out from beneath the earth, clawed the ground to free them and decreed that these people would forever be hunters and gatherers, like the wolf.

We read and hear more history of the settlers' enemies, like the Comanches and Apaches, than we do the Tonkawas, who were as friendly as a tribe was ever going to be toward a people who took their land and wouldn't give it back. We hear a lot about Quanah Parker and how, after his people's defeat, he walked the white man's road with style and dignity. We don't hear a lot about Tonkawa chief Placido, who has been called "the best friend Anglo Texas ever had."

The Tonkawas were an amalgamation of a lot of former independent bands, including the Mayeyes, Yojaunes, Ervipiames and others. Various accounts of the day refer to them as Tonkewega, Tanacoye and Tonquay. A lot of settlers and soldiers simply referred to them as "Tonks."

The governments of the Republic of Texas and later the United States tried to convince the Tonkawas to switch to agriculture as a means of supporting themselves, but that was not the Tonkawa way. The wolf had decreed that they be hunters and gatherers, after all, and they preferred that way of life until the bitter end. Explorer Jean Louis Berlandier reported in 1830 that the Tonkawas could "endure hunger better than any human beings I have ever known." They were said to be extremely fleet afoot and could walk or run long distances without ill effects.

PLACIDO, A TONKAWA CHIEF.

Tonkawa chief Placido was a friend to both white settlers and the army but was nevertheless sent to a reservation, where he was killed. *Library of Congress.*

When hunting and gathering was no longer a realistic option, the Tonkawas took to trading, and they had a certain talent for it. Carita, a particularly shrewd Tonkawa chief, once bragged to Stephen F. Austin that he could cheat Austin out of his entire colony if only Austin would consent to trade with him. Austin was pretty shrewd himself; he declined the offer.

Though early settlers had mixed feelings toward the tribe, generally ranging from disgust to pity, the Tonkawas managed to make themselves useful during the years of the Republic of Texas. Placido formed an alliance with General Edward Burleson that sustained the tribe through the turbulent years of the republic.

At the Battle of Plum Creek in 1840, Placido and thirteen of his Tonkawa scouts, along with Texas militia from Bastrop and Gonzales, bushwhacked a Comanche raiding party near present-day Lockhart and were key to the Texans' victory, but it wasn't enough to keep the Tonkawas in official favor. An 1852 act by the U.S. legislature created a reservation for the Tonkawas at Fort Belknap. If the Tonkawas ever had any real ambition toward agriculture as a way of life, two years of drought and grasshoppers at Fort Belknap did away with those aspirations.

With nothing left to hunt and gather, and plainly failures at agriculture, the Tonkawas were more than willing to accompany Captain John S. ("Rip") Ford in 1858 on an expedition against a Comanche encampment in Oklahoma. The expedition out of Texas onto Indian lands was in direct violation of federal law and a number of treaties, but Ford countered that he was more interested in finding the marauding Indians than learning geography. After the battle, usually referred to as the Battle of Little Robe Creek, Ford had this to say about his Tonkawa allies: "These Indians were men of more than ordinary intellect who possessed minute information concerning the geography and topography of that country—all of Texas, most of Mexico, and all of the Indian territory and adjacent regions."

The *Austin State Gazette* editorialized that Placido be given some cows for his heroic efforts, referring to him as "faithful and industrious." Governor Runnels chimed in that the Texans' "brave Indian allies…will be held in grateful remembrance by the people of Texas." It didn't work out quite that way.

The Tonkawas, including Placido, were removed to a reservation in Oklahoma in 1859. Placido reportedly "cried like a child" when he was left to the care of the Indian agent at the Washita Agency. Maybe he knew what was coming. In October 1862, a group of Delawares, Osages and Shawnees joined with other Indians from the Fort Cobb Agency and attacked the Washita Agency. More than half the Tonkawas were killed, including Placido. The survivors, including Placido's son, Charlie, fled to Fort Griffin in Texas and stayed there until the federal government moved them to Fort Oakland in Oklahoma in 1885.

Today, most of the tribe lives on that reservation and operates the Native Lights Casino on U.S. Highway 77 near the Kansas border. It's not hunting and gathering in the traditional sense, but it's something.

ENCHANTED ROCK

Even when the West was young and wild, Enchanted Rock was old and weird. It has been here about a billion years and isn't going anywhere anytime soon. It is our very own Rock of Ages. Its glitter is said to be the ghost spirits of Comanche warriors. It moans and creaks at night, which the Comanches attributed to evil spirits. It serves as the backdrop for many stories, some of them true. It has been a topic of discussion for about eleven thousand years, which is how long humans have been coming to the rock.

In geologic terms, Enchanted Rock is a batholith—an underground rock formation exposed by erosion. Stone Mountain in Georgia is the largest batholith in the country. Enchanted Rock is the second largest. Enchanted Rock was formed about one billion years ago, when the earth was just a toddler, after two land masses collided. Sediment wedges were mutilated by the collision and superheated from deep within the earth's crust. Those old crystalline forms were now something else, and they rose toward the surface. The magma cooled as it rose, eventually creating a hard granite bubble. That leaves out another episode of continental drift, the emergence of a new ocean, more collisions between busy continents, mountain ranges worn down by millions of years of erosion, more continental drifting and rumbling and a host of other geologic processes, but that's the bumper sticker version of a billion-year-old story.

Enchanted Rock was the setting for many Native American stories and legends. One tells of how a band of warriors were killed on the rock in much the same spirit as would be the defenders of the Alamo

Enchanted Rock has been around a long time and has the stories and legends to prove it. *Leroy Williamson.*

later. An Indian princess is said to have hurled herself from the rock in despair after seeing her people slaughtered by another tribe. Another old chief was thought to walk the domed rock for eternity after sacrificing his daughter. The small depressions that dot the rock were believed to be the chief's footsteps.

One of the earliest written descriptions of the rock came in 1834 from W.B. Dewees, who described the rock as "a large rock of metal which has for many years been considered a wonder. It is supposed to be platinum. The Indians have held it sacred for years, and go there once a year to worship it. It is almost impossible to make any impression on it with chisel and hammers. When struck it gives forth a ringing sound which can be heard for miles around. The party was successful in finding the rock, but were unable to break off any specimens to bring home."

The story you hear most often is how Captain John Coffee Hays got cut off from his company of fellow Texas Rangers and single-handedly fought off a Comanche war party from the rock's considerable vantage point. Some stories have it that the Indians wouldn't tread on the sacred rock to do battle, and other stories credited Hays's unerring marksmanship for the deed. The legends of the rock are so strong and persistent as to be almost etched there as part of the state's collective memory.

Our fascination with the rock continued into the twentieth century. Governor Dan Moody proclaimed it "Texas' most wonderful summer resort" in 1929, two years after owner Tate Moss opened it to the public. The Nature Conservancy took control of the rock and the land around it in 1978. The state bought it and opened it as a state natural area in 1984. It now draws more than 300,000 visitors a year and can be considered a secret all over the state.

Science has put to rest some of the old legends. The glitter the Comanches thought were caused by ghost fires? It's the way granite glitters when the light is just right. On clear nights after a rain, the sparkling, or glittering, is believed to be caused by water trapped in the rock's indentations or by moonlight reflected off wet feldspar. The most considered opinions on why it creaks and moans has it that the rock soaks up a lot of heat from the sun during the day (it does) and creaks and moans—or maybe it sighs—when it cools at night. However, old Charles

Moss is said to have spent a thousand or more nights at the base of the rock and never heard a peep out of it.

That doesn't mean that Enchanted Rock doesn't have a lot of stories to tell. You just won't hear them from the rock itself—unless, of course, you do.

LLANO GOLD

There was a time in the late 1880s when the people of the Texas Hill Country came down with a collective and fairly severe case of gold fever. The Klondike gold rush to Alaska was still very much in the news, and the prospect of a possible gold strike made people pay attention to the rocks and formations of the land. Maybe they knew that not everything that glitters is gold, but some of it is and it doesn't hurt anything to be vigilant in one's observations. Finding the right kind of glitter on your land was the frontier equivalent of striking oil or winning the lottery.

The fever was fueled by a couple of insignificant finds that at least one newspaper of the day played for a lot more than they were worth. The *Kansas City Journal* announced in its February 7, 1888 issue that "Texans are trying to realize the startling fact that they have a Klondike in their very own midst."

The main subject of the story was the Mount Hudson Mine just east of Willow City in northeast Gillespie County. A prospector, identified in the Kansas City paper as a veteran of western gold camps, spied Hudson Mountain one day and thought that it reminded him of similar formations he had seen in Colorado. He found some of the color he was looking for—gold—in an inch-wide stream of quartz on the mountain. A sample was assayed at seventy-three dollars in gold to the ton. The prospector kept digging until his money ran out, and then he recruited investors to form the Mount Hudson Mining Company.

Initial results were promising and word got out. "The strike in the Mount Hudson Mine is of such a remarkable character in both the richness and the extent of the ore body as to leave no further doubt of the existence of a great gold-bearing belt in that country. Already a tangible project is on foot to give this city direct communication with the new gold fields," the *Kansas City Star* declared.

The *New York Times* apparently sent a correspondent to the area to check out the claims in the Kansas City paper. In its March 20 edition, the *Times* ran a headline that read "Fortunes Sunk in Mines" and "Llano District a Big Hoax."

The *Times* reporter noted that some of the ore mined in the area assayed rich in gold but that not one vein of gold had been discovered. He went to see A.C. Schryver of San Antonio, who was the first person to sink significant money and labor into exploring the region for gold. Schryver said that he had found some nice pockets of ore but so far not even a single vein. "He says that a true vein of gold ore has not been found in the whole Llano district, and that until such a vein is discovered it can never become a valuable mining region," the story noted.

The reporter also talked to H.D. Merford, who had spent considerable time learning about gold and looking for it. Merford wasn't too impressed with the prospects in the region, but he noted that prospectors were still flocking to the Hill Country. "I found the district full of prospectors and the people of the towns of Sabinal, Uvalde, Fredericksburg and Llano are worked up to a high fever pitch of excitement over the alleged gold finds," Merford said. "Nearly every man I met up in that country had a little bottle of yellow sand and an imaginary nugget of gold to show me. This excitement is entirely unwarranted and I would certainly advise men of money to go slow until further and more conclusive developments are made."

The *Times* also suggested another reason that you don't hear of a lot of Texans getting rich from finding gold. "Texas laws are such that the poor prospector has no show whatsoever," Merford said, adding that Texas law had it that if a rich strike should be made, the landowner would also own the mine.

The excitement over gold soon faded in the Hill Country, which is apt to happen when precious little gold is found. Some gold was found at Sharp Mountain in Llano County, but geologists concluded that the gold was volcanic in origin, meaning that the vein that produced it was several thousand feet underground.

Gold fever quietly faded away in the Texas Hill Country, though the rich deposits of other rocks and minerals have continued to play a key role in the development of the region for many years to follow.

BARRINGER HILL

No one was exactly yelling out, "There's yttrium in them thar hills!" when the rare mineral was discovered in Llano County in the late 1880s. No one other than a few scientists and businessmen had ever even heard of the stuff, but it turned out to be the most valuable mineral ever discovered in the county. An ounce of the stuff sold for $144 per pound in 1887, a year in which gold went for $19 on the London exchange.

Attempts to find gold in the otherwise mineral-rich region had come to naught, but the Hill Country had come down with a case of gold fever anyway. People were apt to do a little prospecting on their land when they could—because you just never know. One such person was John Barringer. A hill—actually more of a mound than a hill—located on his property was known Barringer Hill. While doing a little prospecting there one day, he found a heavy green-black outcropping that he hadn't seen before. A geologist, professor and tireless booster of Llano, N.J. Badu, sent samples to Philadelphia and New York for analysis; the rock was determined to be gadolinite, which would soon be used as a filament in streetlamps of the day.

This discovery brought two of the country's greatest inventors, Thomas Edison and George Westinghouse, into the mix. Both men were looking for gadolinite, and the discovery in Llano County caught their attention because the only other known sources were in Russia and Norway. About half of gadolinite is composed of yttrium, which was used in early pre-incandescent electric lights.

A young mineralogist named William Niven was sent to Llano County to see how much gadolinite might be available there. In Llano County, Niven found himself in a sort of mineral wonderland. He discovered forty-seven minerals in the area, including five that were new to science. He paid Barringer either $5,000 or $10,000 in gold for the hill in the name of the Piedmont Mining Company, which began serious operations there in 1902. That was about the time the incandescent light bulb was invented, which made yttrium essentially worthless.

The man who had to deliver the bad news to the miners was a bright young engineer named Marshall Hanks, who had discovered how to use yttrium to improve the life of the old Nernst streetlights from a couple of hours to more than seven hundred hours. This accomplishment might

Barringer Hill wasn't much to look at, but it was at one time the site of the world's largest deposit of rare earthen minerals.

have made Hanks a respected member of the scientific community, but it did nothing to endear him to the miners who worked for him at the Piedmont mine.

Hanks reportedly came to the area with a preconceived notion of Texans as nothing more than scoundrels and murderers. The miners did their best to reinforce that stereotype, and the young engineer was said to be the butt of many a prank meant to scare the daylights out of him.

Part of the locals' aversion to Hanks also centered on his tendency to keep secrets from them, such as the nature of the rocks and minerals that they handled on a daily basis. Since Hanks didn't tell them what they were mining, many assumed that they were handling radium and demanded hazard pay. In fact, many of the rocks found at Barringer Hill *were* radioactive. When the newfangled incandescent light bulb was invented, Westinghouse sent word to Hanks that he was to close the mine. The news was either greeted with great anger or with a sense of levity, depending on which version of the story you believe.

Some accounts of Hanks's last days in Llano County play it straight and insist that Hanks's being shipped out of town hidden in a crate of ore bound for Pennsylvania was part of a real-life desperate attempt to get out of town alive. Others recount the episode as a prank, which is probably more likely.

Someone watching the events unfold, as in a documentary film, would see the angry miners descend on the Wells Fargo agent in charge of shipping the ore by train. The angry mob of miners confront the agent and demand that the crates of ore be turned over to them for inspection, just in case the man they want to kill, Marshall Hanks, happens to be in one of them. The agent, who has just finished nailing shut a crate that contains the terrified Hanks, turns the mob away by threatening them with the full power at Wells Fargo's command if anything should happen to even one of those crates.

Either way—prank or true escape—Hanks believed that he had escaped certain death by the skin of his teeth. The crate in which he traveled out of town was opened when the train was out of Llano County, and Hanks was set free.

Rock hounds and geologists still visited Barringer Hill after the mine closed, but all that came to a halt in 1937 when the land was flooded to create Lake Buchanan, closing the books on one of the world's richest deposits of rare minerals.

CHARCOAL BURNERS AND CEDAR CHOPPERS

The tree that nearly everybody calls cedar is really Ashe juniper, except when it's another kind of juniper or cedar. Nearly everybody knows this, but the tree is still and will most likely always be referred to as cedar, as will be the case here. The cedar is native to the Hill Country and central Texas, but it hasn't always been as native as it is now. That is to say, there is a lot more of it now than there used to be, and that's not necessarily a good thing, because there was plenty of it to begin with.

Overgrazing of pastures had a lot to do with the proliferation of cedar. Ranchers also burned the prairies and cleared away the cedar, allowing shorter and more nourishing grasses to take their place. As the number of trees declined, excess runoff from rains made the soils too shallow to support very much grass. That cleared the way for brush and trees to take over the landscape; the cedar was back to stay. The dreaded Cedar

Fever—an allergy to cedar pollen—that so plagues susceptible central Texans today was a problem in days of yore, but with more people and more cedar, the incidence is higher. "We didn't have time to get cedar fever," one old-timer groused.

At a time when the majority of people made their living from the land in one form or another, the cedar brakes were always there to be exploited. One of the earliest uses of the cedar was the burning of it to make charcoal, which was used to heat stoves and flatirons of the day. A hotbed of this kind of activity was located along the banks of the Guadalupe River from about New Braunfels to Sisterdale, an area that came to be known as Charcoal City. German settlers first discovered the market for charcoal and took to burning it during the time between planting and harvest. By the 1880s, charcoal burners from Georgia, Tennessee, Indiana, New York and even Ireland and England had made their way into the Guadalupe valley and were turning cedar into cash.

Cedar brakes like this one provided the raw material for the charcoal burners and cedar choppers of the Hill Country. *Author photo.*

The cedars were cut while they were still green to ensure a slow burn and then chopped into poles and the bark peeled away. Two or three cords of wood were arranged in a pyramid in a kiln or pit and then covered with dirt. A hole was left at the top of the stack, tepee-style, to allow smoke to escape. A hole at the bottom was closed up after the fire was lit. After that, the charcoal burner had to "hurry up and wait" for the fire to do its work, which usually took a few days. The Guadalupe valley became sort of the Smoky Mountains of Texas as a haze of smoke, redolent of cedar, hung over the valley for much of the year. Flare-ups had to be extinguished quickly with dirt or water, or else the cedar would burn into ash rather than smoldering into charcoal. When the cedar was charred to perfection, the fire was put out and the charcoal raked into sacks, put on wagons and hauled into town.

The best markets for Hill Country charcoal were San Antonio and Austin, so most of the burners loaded their wagons with charcoal and hauled them to those towns. J. Frank Dobie recalled hearing the burners call out "Char-r-coal" as they drove their wagons through Austin in 1914. A wagonload brought from eight to twenty-four dollars, depending on supply and how many burners might be cut off from the market by high waters at a time when there weren't a lot of bridges and the Hill Country rivers ran undammed and untamed. Still, charcoal was money in the pocket any time of year and could be counted on when corn and cotton failed.

Opportunities for the charcoal burner diminished quickly after World War I. Not only did the Hill Country have bridges by that time, but railroads also had long since arrived and the Model T truck made it possible to carry cedar posts to market without going to all the trouble of turning it into charcoal first. Use of charcoal-heated flatirons had decreased too, and the development of barbed wire fences created a great demand for cedar posts. That cleared the way for that unique Hill Country character, the cedar chopper.

One of the ironic consequences of the rapid proliferation of cedar is that the fabled character type known to generations as the cedar chopper has all but disappeared at a time when cedar has prospered and multiplied.

Cedar choppers were, as their tag suggests, people who chopped cedar for a living. They were independent contractors—and independent in about every other way, too. Cedar, even in the early days of settlement, was heavy in certain areas of the state, especially in the Hill Country and along the Colorado and Brazos River Bottoms. Most of the cedar fence posts you see in the Hill Country today were fashioned by the sweat of a cedar chopper's brow. A Palo Pinto County historian, writing in 1946, noted that "the chopper who cuts today and lives in the cedar is as true a mountaineer as his forefathers, who perhaps hailed from the Ozarks or the Blue Ridge Mountains in pioneer days. He has not been noticeably touched by what is known as present day civilization."

While calling someone a cedar chopper is sometimes used as a slur—like calling them a hillbilly, hick or rube—it is hard not to admire the independence that so marked their lives. They did a day's work and got a day's pay, usually on the same day. The chopper could work all day, half a day or not at all, depending on his preference and how much money was needed to get him through that particular day.

Those who perhaps envied the cedar chopper's freedom from convention were also apt to call him lazy. It's a safe bet that most of the people who cast those aspersions never spent a summer afternoon in the cedar brake with an axe. The cedar brake wasn't a place for the lazy or the weak. It was the domain of the cedar chopper and all that lived there, including snakes.

Walter J. Cartwright, writing in the November 1966 issue of the *Southwest Historical Quarterly*, noted that snakes and runaway trucks were the most common hazards facing cedar choppers. Stories of runaway trucks kept appearing in his research. "To remove the big posts, a chopper frequently must drive an old truck over sizable hills and gullies along a lane cleared by the axe and chain saw. If its brakes fail, nothing stops the truck until it reaches the bottom of the hill," he wrote.

Texas writer Roy Bedichek wrote eloquently in *Adventures with a Texas Naturalist* of encountering a cedar chopper along the banks of the Pedernales River. Bedichek admired the old man's skill with the axe and stopped to chat with him a moment. The man told Bedichek that he was cutting cedar because he was eighty-six years old and that was all he had ever done since he was ten years old. He didn't need the money, but he kept chopping away because a neighbor of his had put away his axe and been bedridden ever since. He didn't want that to happen to him.

"He thought he might die soon anyway and that it was better to keep doing something," Bedichek wrote. "This is the pioneer philosophy of being up and doing, of marching on to the end of the row, of never quitting. It is the gospel of salvation by work." It is not the gospel of a lazy man.

Like their charcoal-burning ancestors, the cedar chopper has all but disappeared from the scene, but the cedar is still very much with us.

White Gold

Aside from the soldiers and supplies that Texas contributed to the Confederacy, the state's most important contribution to the Civil War might have been the salt that was processed at various locations in the state, including a saltworks in Llano County. While the Confederacy lasted, the place was known as the Confederate Salt Works. Before that, it was the Bluffton-Tow Salt Works, because it was located between those two communities.

This matter of salt might not seem so important in a world in which we buy it by the box and toss it over our shoulder for good luck if we happen to spill some. But salt was an important commodity in the Civil War, right up there with ammunition. The Civil War is sometimes called the War Between the Salts. The North had plenty of salt; the South did not. The Union won the war. "Salt is eminently contraband, because of its use in curing meats, without which armies cannot be subsisted," wrote Union general William Tecumseh Sherman in 1862.

The South could not be subsisted, as the general would have it. By 1865, when the Southern cause was clearly lost, the Confederate manual had this bit of advice for its soldiers: "To keep meat from spoiling in the summer, eat it early in the spring."

Civil War soldiers, horses and mules all depended on salt. So did the livestock. If an army travels on its stomach, as the saying goes, that army better have plenty of salt. Salt was also used as a medical disinfectant. Napoleon lost many soldiers to otherwise simple wounds because his army had run out of salt.

Salt was one of the world's earliest precious commodities. The earliest trade routes were established in response to a demand for the stuff. Jericho was established almost ten thousand years ago as a salt trading center. Salt was worth its weight in gold during the Middle Ages, traded weight for weight. The English word "salary" comes from the Latin word "salarium," which was a soldier's pay in salt. A good soldier or hired hand was said to be "worth his salt." Homer called it a "divine substance."

Not that Texans ever needed to be convinced of salt's importance. The Chisholm Trail zigzagged like it did not only to find watering holes but also to take advantage of salt licks. Before there was the "black gold" of the oil boom, there was the "white gold" that salt represented. The people of San Elizaro and other villages along the Rio Grande River near El Paso used a salt basin in northeastern Hudspeth County as a road to transport salt. When Anglo politicians claimed ownership and tried to levy fees, war broke out—that old taxation-without-representation thing again.

Local sources of salt became important in Texas after Union raids on saltworks in Florida and Louisiana depleted Confederate supplies. The salt manufactured in Llano County was used for the table, meat preservation, part of the feed rationings for cavalry horses and for tanning hides. Before the creeks and springs were enlisted for the war effort, the area was used by Indians for hundreds of years, most likely as an infirmary and crude sort of day spa. The salt there was from Cambrian Sea waters that had been trapped five hundred million years ago in sand and strata.

David Cowan was one of Llano County's earliest settlers and a surveyor. When friendly Indians in the region gave him permission to survey the area, they told him of a salt bank located along the west bank of the Colorado River. He settled on the bank and began producing salt there in 1852. A day's boiling in one hundred 250-gallon iron kettles produced twenty to thirty bushels of salt. It was cooked, sacked and hauled out to help the Hill Country and Confederacy meet its wartime shortages. The first Llano District Court was held at the saltworks, and there was a stagecoach stop nearby.

The site of the old saltworks has been under the waters of Lake Buchanan since 1935. A historical marker commemorating the saltworks is located at the intersection of State Highway 29 and FM 261.

As innocuous as the marker might be, a case could be made that the most important battle of the Civil War fought on Texas soil was waged at the state's various salines. The Union had salt and the South did not, and in the end, the Union salted away the Confederacy.

CAPITALS OF TEXAS

Before it settled in Austin, the Texas state capital was all over the place. This was especially true during the state's years as a republic, when military commanders of the day thought it best to keep the capital a moving target. At various times, San Felipe, Washington-on-the-Brazos, Harrisburg, Galveston Island, Velasco, Columbia and Houston all had a turn as the center of state government. Subsequently, the people chose sides in a power struggle between factions favoring a city named for Sam Houston or a new city, Waterloo, which President Mirabeau Lamar liked because it was pretty and thick with buffalo.

The republic's provisional government met at Washington-on-the-Brazos on March 1, 1836, at the behest of the town's founders, who were dreadfully unprepared when the offer was accepted. A scheduled three-month convention was cut to seventeen days partly because the little community wasn't ready to be a capital of anything. There was little food except fatback and cornbread, and the buildings had no windows or heat. Just when the delegates were settling down to business, a blue norther blew in.

The new government drafted a declaration of independence at Washington-on-the-Brazos, appointed Sam Houston commander in chief and then found out that Santa Anna had taken the Alamo and was headed east. The delegates left Washington-on-the-Brazos in a hurry and took their capital with them, first to Harrisburg and then to Buffalo Bayou. A steamboat served as site of a de facto state capital when they boarded one to Galveston Island. From there, the capital was located in Velasco.

In May 1837, the capital was moved to Houston, a town founded on the Buffalo Bayou by A.C. Allen and John Kirby and named for Sam Houston. The Allen brothers offered to build a two-story capitol building for free if Houston was made the capital of the republic, and it came to pass—for a while.

Lamar served as Houston's vice-president, but he cared little for Houston the man or Houston the city and decided to take a little vacation from both. Lamar and his secretary, Reverend Edward Fontaine, set out for the frontier, where the Comanches still held sway. They got an escort of six Texas Rangers to a small stockade settlement at the mouth

Houston, named for Sam Houston (above), was one of many capitals of Texas both as a republic and state. *Library of Congress.*

of Shoal Creek called Waterloo. At a site where Congress and Seventh Streets intersect in downtown Austin today, Lamar killed a huge buffalo bull. The party assembled afterward on a hill where the state capitol now stands, and Lamar, stirred by the beauty of the Colorado River

Mirabeau Lamar once killed a buffalo near where Seventh Street and Congress Avenue in Austin intersect today. *Texas State Library.*

Valley, declared that this should be the seat of future empire; Lamar was big on empires.

When Lamar became president of the republic in 1838, one of his first acts was to appoint a commission to locate a site for a new capital closer to the middle of the state. The commission voted unanimously for Waterloo, noting that the Colorado River Valley's "fertile and gracefully undulating woodlands and luxuriant Prairies at a distance from it." This, the commission concluded, was "a region worthy only of being the home of the brave and the free." The Texas Congress approved the measure and renamed the city for Stephen F. Austin, the father of Texas.

The Comanches, who had called the land their home ever since running out the Apaches, retreated south and west of Austin, into the Texas Hill Country, and exacted a terrible revenge on Anglo settlers trying to make a living from that beautiful but sometimes forbidding land.

Sam Houston, in his second term as president of the republic, ordered the capital back to Houston when Mexican troops again menaced the city of San Antonio. This did not go over well with the people of Austin. Officials settled on Washington-on-the-Brazos as a compromise, while Houston sent a group of rangers to get the archives in Austin and fetch them back to Houston. He stipulated, however, that the retrieval be bloodless. A group opposing the move was unprepared for the rangers' raid on the state archives, though Mrs. Angelina Eberly fired a cannon at Houston's men as they departed. The vigilantes took off in armed pursuit and caught up with the rangers and the archives at Kenney's Fort on Brushy Creek. The rangers put up token resistance before turning the archives over to the angry Austinites.

The constitution of 1845 provided that Austin be the state capital until 1850, at which time an election would be held to decide the site of a permanent capital. Austin won that election with 7,674 votes. The 1845 document also called for another election, just in case Austin didn't work out. Austin won the subsequent election with 63,297 votes, followed by Houston with 35,188 and Waco with 12,776.

The first supposedly permanent capitol building burned down in 1881 and was replaced with the present structure in May 1888.

Part II

THE GOOD, THE BAD AND THE WITTY

WILD RAM OF THE MOUNTAINS

If Lyman Wight could have had his way, Texas and not Utah might have become home to the Church of Jesus Christ of Latter Day Saints and the Mormon Church. Wight brought about 150 fellow Mormons across the Red River into Texas in November 1845. They spent the winter in Grayson County and, in the spring of 1846, migrated south to a spot near present-day Webberville.

They chose that site because Wight said that the recently slain Mormon leader Joseph Smith had told him to build a new colony there, on the Colorado River, where Tom Miller Dam is today. They built a mill, but it was soon washed away by a flood. That, combined with a generally cool reception from the people in Travis County, led Wight to move his group to the Pedernales River near Fredericksburg, where they founded the town of Zodiac.

The Mormons received a more favorable reception among the German settlers of Gillespie County, who respected their hard work and enterprise. The Mormons built the county's first sawmill, along with a new gristmill, temple, school and store—all within the first six months of arriving. Wight even managed to get along with the Comanche chief Buffalo Hump, thus helping to maintain an uneasy peace.

This replica of Lyman Wight's water wheel in Fredericksburg pays tribute to Wight and his band of early Mormon settlers. *Author photo.*

Wight had followed a rocky path to Texas. Along with Joseph Smith, he was among the nine Mormons who were tried for treason and other crimes against the state in Missouri. Their incarceration eventually turned into a political embarrassment, and they were allowed to escape.

Wight was elected to the Quorum of 12 Apostles, which directs the activities of the Latter Day Saints (LDS) church. He ran a Wisconsin sawmill for a time and then traveled the country campaigning for Smith, who was running for president. After Smith and his brother Hyrum were murdered by a mob in Illinois, Brigham Young was chosen to lead the church.

Wight was called the "Wild Ram of the Mountains" because of his generally rebellious nature and stubborn independence. That nature was evident in his reaction to Young's leadership, which he refused to accept. He gathered his followers and took off to Texas, like he said Smith had told him to do.

The Zodiac community was unlike anything people in the Hill County had seen before. While the other settlers appreciated the group's hardworking ways, other peculiarities rankled them. Polygamy, which Wight and the Mormons preached and practiced, was particularly vexing. Nor was Wight faring any better with those of his own faith. Brigham Young dispatched a couple of missionaries to Texas with the expressed purpose of bringing Wight back to Utah and into the Mormon fold, but Wight refused. He was excommunicated.

Wight stayed at Zodiac; he ran for chief justice of Gillespie County in 1850 and lost but took over the office after he pointed out that his opponent, Johann Jost Klingelhoefer, hadn't yet been granted American citizenship. Klingelhoefer took over a short while later after Wight stopped attending county court sessions.

Wight's group, which usually numbered about 175, moved to Burnet County after another flood destroyed the mill at Zodiac. The Mormon Mill Colony became as busy and productive as the previous settlements had been but, like those ventures, was not very profitable. The group conducted its business apart from the rest of the county, which increased resentment from other settlers.

Not everybody held the Mormons in disdain. Noah Smithwick, who bought their Burnet County mill after the group moved to Bandera County, was skeptical of some of the "miracles" and "visions" that Wight and some of the others claimed to have had. He wrote of them: "I found them just the same as other people in matters of business. While some of them were honest and industrious, others were shiftless and unreliable; and this must prove a potent argument against community holdings—the thriftless got as much as the thrifty…Nor was there anything objectionable in the Mormons as neighbors. If there were any polygamous families, I did not know of them."

The place where Wight and his followers settled in Bandera County was called Mormon Camp and is covered now by the waters of Medina Lake. Wight performed the first marriage ceremony in Bandera County when he did the honors for his son Levi Lamoni and Sophia Leyland. He determined to leave Texas because he suspected that a war between the North and the South over the issue of slavery would soon take place. Wight, who was passionate in his opposition to slavery, prepared to lead his followers back to Missouri, but on the second day of the journey, he suffered a heart attack and died. He was buried at the Mormon cemetery in Zodiac.

The majority of Texas Mormons went to Galland's Grove, Iowa, which is considered a landmark move in the Reorganized Mormon Church. Some of them stayed behind. Three of Wight's sons stayed and fought for the South in the Civil War.

BLIND MAN'S TOWN

They called the man who founded Marble Falls "Stovepipe" because of a sneaky trick he pulled off as a Confederate commander in the Civil War. The town he founded was called Blind Man's Town because he was blind when he laid out the streets of the town by memory.

Adam "Stovepipe" Rankin Johnson came to Texas from Kentucky in 1854 at age twenty and settled in Hamilton Valley in Burnet County, but he rambled far and wide. A surveyor by trade, he surveyed much of west Texas before any vestiges of civilization had arrived there. He ranged from Buffalo Gap in today's Taylor County and ventured west of the Pecos River long before Judge Roy Bean instituted his peculiar brand of law and order in the region. He transported goods and animals to isolated Butterfield Overland Mail stations. The young Adam R. Johnson got around.

Johnson first saw his future home in 1854 when he rode down the Colorado River from Fort Mason to see the "great falls," which were also called the "marble falls." The falls, which are covered now by the waters of Lake Marble Falls, are located just upriver from the present U.S. Highway 281 Bridge in Marble Falls and can occasionally still be seen when the Lower Colorado River Authority lowers the water level for repairs. At the time, they were a dominant feature of the area.

Johnson, who became the city's first surveyor, was intrigued by the idea of harnessing the power of the Colorado to power mills and factories. He thought that Shirley Shoals, west of Burnet, was a perfect site. (A century later, that would be the exact site of Buchanan Dam.) Just when he was ready to act on his notions, the Civil War started. He married Josephine Eastland in 1861 and then went back to Kentucky and signed up as a scout under General Nathan Bedford Forrest, rising through the ranks to become a brigadier general.

Johnson gained the nickname "Stovepipe" when his group of twelve captured Newburgh, Indiana, from a much larger Union force by

The Marble Falls, located near the town of the same name, was a landmark and the site of many a business plan until they were covered up by the waters of Lake Marble Falls. *Library of Congress.*

mounting two stovepipes on wagon wheels to make the Union troops think that they would be going to be up against some heavy artillery. In 1864, Johnson led a charge against Union soldiers in Kentucky and was accidentally shot by one of his own men. Such was the nature of the Civil War that his soldiers decided to leave Johnson on the battlefield in hopes that Union surgeons would be able to save his life. The Federal doctors did indeed save his life but not his vision. (There was some confusion about that, and several Southern newspapers actually ran his obituary fifty-eight years prematurely.)

Back in Marble Falls, Johnson opened a land office and a home he called Airy Mount that still stands today. He had his young son drive him in a buggy to various spots to conduct business, guided by memory and a private vision of what the new town would look like. He obtained financing for a cotton operation and laid out a water system and a hydraulic power plant; as was the case with most things built on central Texas rivers in those days, it was washed away by a flood.

Johnson set about having the plant rebuilt, this time utilizing tapered granite walls, but the project was never completed. Johnson also founded the Texas Mining Improvement Company; via $700 and the granting of a seven-mile right-of-way, he was able to get the railroad spur that he believed the town desperately needed if it was to prosper. His grant and cash also allowed the state to haul granite from Granite Mountain for construction of the new state capitol building in Austin. Johnson died at Burnet in 1922. His funeral services were held in the Senate Chamber of the state capitol, and he was buried in the State Cemetery.

One of Johnson's sons became known as Adam Rankin Johnson Sr. but was called Tex Johnson when he pitched in baseball's Major Leagues in 1914 and 1915 and again in 1918. He also played with the Chicago Whales and Baltimore Terrapins of the old Federal League. Though technically he should have been called Adam Rankin Johnson Jr., that name was given to his son, who was born in Arizona (probably during spring training) but spent most of his formative years in the Burnet and Marble Falls area. Johnson Jr. made a career of baseball, eventually becoming president of the Eastern League.

As for Marble Falls, it grew and prospered and is today a popular Hill Country recreation spot. We have to think that the blind man would be proud of his town if he could see it now.

THE FIRST WAR CORRESPONDENT

The man for whom Kendall County is named is credited with being America's first war correspondent and the father of the sheep business in Texas. Even without those notations in the state's history, we would know him as a survivor and chronicler of the ill-fated Santa Fe Expedition.

George W. Kendall was born in New England, where he learned the printing trade and drifted south, eventually ending up in New Orleans and founding the *New Orleans Picayune*, a daily newspaper often described as "a saucy little sheet which sold for the price of a Spanish coin called a picayune that was worth 6¼ cents."

Kendall took on the role of correspondent and signed up for what sounded like a good story and a rousing adventure: an expedition to Santa Fe that would claim New Mexico for Texas. Mirabeau Lamar, the second president of the Republic of Texas, sent the men on their way via his version of Manifest Destiny despite the fact that Congress hadn't signed off on the deal. The story took an ugly turn when Lamar's soldiers of fortune were captured by Mexican authorities and marched off to Mexico City, where they were imprisoned in a leper colony.

Out of that experience came Kendall's first book, *Narratives of the Texas Santa Fe Expedition*. The book was a bestseller and remains in print today. J. Frank Dobie considered the book "journalistically verbose," but most critics give it high marks as one of the best campaign narratives ever written.

Kendall was eventually released from prison and made his way back to New Orleans, where his book was serialized in the *Picayune*. He used the newspaper to drum up support for a war with Mexico, and when that came to pass he served as a correspondent, riding and reporting with Ben McCullough's Texas Rangers and as an aide de camp to General William Worth, for whom Fort Worth is named.

Kendall used the Pony Express along with ships and the telegraph to get his stories back to New Orleans, immortalizing himself in the process as the country's first true war correspondent. He was on the scene when McCullough's troops stormed Monterrey, and he was there at the landing of Veracruz and the Mexico City campaign. A book about his experiences in the war with Mexico also sold briskly. Kendall went to Europe and met his wife-to-be, Adeline de Valcourt, in France. The couple lived in that country for several years; it was in France where Kendall started studying sheep breeding and raising in earnest.

Six years after the Kendalls moved to Texas, George bought the Post Oak Ranch near Boerne in 1861 and did much to promote and expand the sheep industry. In a sketch of Kendall written for the National Society of the Daughters of the American Revolution, Frances Lipe noted that "the greatest innovation Kendall gave to the sheep industry was crossbreeding the Mexican Churro ewes with the fine-fleeced Merinos, to produce a new strain with the stamina needed for the Texas hill country and the fine wool of the Merinos. Not only were they prolific in breeding, but they increased wool production dramatically. He found that the local Germans made excellent shepherds. He paid them in sheep and taught them the skills of sheep ranching. Thus, they built the sheep industry to its present day huge proportions in this area."

Kendall kept writing, including some reminiscences of his colorful life on the frontier, but mostly he wrote about sheep, including a book on sheep husbandry written with business partner Henry S. Randall.

After Kendall died of pneumonia in 1867, Randall wrote of him:

> *He loved Texas with an absolute devotion. He never was tired of writing or speaking in its praise. He loved its vast expanses of solitude, its majestic plains, its noble rivers, the green hills of the county named after him, and its masculine energetic population.*
>
> *George Wilkins Kendall earned his place as the father of the Texas sheep industry through hard work and energetic promotion of that industry. He did Texas and the sheep industry a great service.*

Through his writing, particularly his account of the Santa Fe Expedition, Kendall did Texas history a great service as well.

THE STEAMBOAT HOTEL

Life wasn't always rough on the frontier. People who stayed at the Nimitz Hotel in Fredericksburg in the last half of the twentieth century found a welcome respite from the challenges of the wilderness that surrounded the town. Here they could stay at a hotel with a bathhouse, a brewery, gardens and a music hall. Such were the definitions of luxury.

Charles Henry Nimitz, who came to America with his family from Germany when he was eighteen, made his way from Charleston, South Carolina, to Fredericksburg on the first wagon train to that town in 1846. Despite his tender years, Nimitz had been around. He had served in the German merchant marines from the time he was fourteen until he came to America. He worked briefly as a bookkeeper in Fredericksburg and served for a time with the Texas Rangers in 1851. A year later, he built his hotel.

Depending on which way a traveler was heading, the Nimitz was the last real hotel on a stagecoach line that ran from San Diego to San Antonio, the longest line in the country at that time. The Nimitz was often called the Steamboat Hotel after Nimitz added a steamboat-shaped superstructure, complete with a bridge and crow's nest, in the 1880s. The addition was a nostalgic nod to his younger days spent on the high seas.

Almost everybody who was anybody who traveled through Fredericksburg stayed at the Nimitz. Its guest registry contained, at

The Nimitz Hotel was a welcome oasis on the Hill Country frontier. *Mike and Nancy Kelsey Collection.*

various times, President Rutherford B. Hayes, Robert E. Lee, Ulysses S. Grant and the man who urged a generation to "Go West, young man," Horace Greeley. A young bank teller from Austin, William Sydney Porter, who would go on to lasting fame as a writer under the name O. Henry, spent some time there and set one of his short stories, "A Chaparral Prince," in Fredericksburg.

The hard times of the Civil War cramped the hotel's style considerably. The "coffee" of that era was a concoction of parched sweet potatoes and toasted barley. The hotel brewery had to serve as a cistern. To make matters worse, Nimitz supported the Confederacy, which put him in the minority in Gillespie County. He organized the Gillespie Rifles, a frontier guard unit, and was commissioned as a captain in the Confederacy by John S. Ford, who commanded the frontier district.

Nimitz had more trouble from the Confederate "loyalists" in the Hill Country than he did from the Union sympathizers in his midst. A group that came to be known as Die Haengebande (the Hangman's Band) terrorized the countryside in the name of the Confederacy, which did little to endear citizens to their cause. When Nimitz sent conscription orders to the men, they responded by storming the hotel with the sole purpose of hanging Nimitz, who found refuge in the brewery-cistern. The leader of the band, J.P. Waldrip, was shot to death by an unknown assassin not far from the hotel in 1867. Most of the other gang members were eventually indicted for their activities. In 1890, Nimitz served as a state representative from District 89, which included Gillespie, Comal and Blanco Counties. He deeded the hotel to his son, Charles H. Nimitz Jr., in 1906 and lived at the hotel until his death in 1911.

Chester H. Nimitz, his grandson, was born in 1885. His father, Chester Bernard Nimitz, died before he was born; his mother later married her husband's younger brother, William Nimitz. During those early years, Chester spent a considerable amount of time in his grandfather's company at the hotel and learned to "walk the corridors as though he were on the deck of a ship." He dropped out of high school in Kerrville but scored high on a competitive examination to be admitted to the U.S. Naval Academy at Annapolis, from which he graduated 7th in a class of 114 in 1905.

Nimitz, who also served the navy in World War I, rose through the ranks and took command of the Pacific fleet in the wake of Japan's attack on Pearl Harbor on December 7, 1941. He engineered the strategies that held the Japanese at bay and eventually resulted in the Battle of Midway, which historians credit with turning the tide of war in the favor of American and its allies. Chester Nimitz once said that his only regret was that his grandfather had not lived to see him become an admiral.

Charles Nimitz Jr. and his wife sold the hotel in 1926 to a group of local men who remodeled it extensively, even removing the battleship superstructure. Henry J. Schmidt eventually took it over and dissolved the corporation that had owned it in 1947. The old hotel closed its doors in 1963, and Schmidt sold it to the Admiral Chester H. Nimitz Naval Museum in 1964. The museum was established as a state agency in 1969. The Sixty-seventh Legislature handed control of the museum to the Texas Parks and Wildlife Department in 1981.

Today, the hotel is the site of three separate museums. The Pacific War Museum is located in the faithfully remodeled Nimitz Steamboat Hotel.

The Japanese Garden of Peace was donated by the people of Japan as bicentennial gift in 1976. The History Walk of the Pacific War traces the Pacific fleet's battles and travails from Pearl Harbor to Tokyo Bay.

In the midst of all of this, you can still find the old bathhouse and the fireplace where the water was heated, completing a circle that extends from before the Civil War to these many years after World War II.

Treu Der Union

Depending on your own interpretation, the Battle of the Nueces was either a bona fide battle or a lopsided massacre. As a battle, it wasn't much. A group of German Americans, fed up with this whole Civil War business, was heading to Mexico when they were attacked by Confederate cavalry. Of the sixty-five or so Unionists who set out for Mexico, thirty-four were either killed at the battle or later captured and killed.

The incident on the Nueces River, about twenty miles from Brackettville, happened on August 10, 1862, and was part of a growing conflict between German Texans and their neighbors. German immigrants had been settling in Texas since the latter days of Mexico's sovereignty. Many of them came because of a strong belief in individual freedom, and the slavery issue did not strike a lot of these people as the proper expression of a freedom-loving people. At the annual *Staats-Saengerfest* meeting in 1845, delegates from the German political club adopted resolutions declaring that slavery was evil and that Texas should get the federal government to help abolish it. Though German sentiment toward Texas's role in the Civil War was diverse and included many who fought for the Confederacy, declarations such as the one in 1845 led to suspicion and downright hostility toward German Americans as the Civil War descended on Texas.

In Comfort, an enclave composed of mostly German intellectuals and freethinkers, news of the impending Civil War and Texas's role as a Confederate state was met with open opposition. Along with like-minded immigrants from Kendall and Gillespie Counties, the men of Comfort formed the Union Loyal League to protect the German settlements not only from Indian raids but also from Confederate attacks. In the days

The men massacred at the Battle of Nueces were not buried until after the Civil War had ended. *Library of Congress.*

following Texas's secession from the Union, many unsuspecting and innocent German farmers were murdered and their farms burned or otherwise destroyed by Confederate renegades. Some reports have it that as many as 150 people were killed in such a manner. Confederate authorities declared Kerr and its contiguous counties—Gillespie, Kendall, Edwards and Kimble—to be in open rebellion and subject to martial law. Texas Rangers were sent to the area to order all males older than sixteen to take an oath of allegiance to the Confederacy.

This continued until the men around Comfort decided that enough was enough. They disbanded the Union Loyal League and on August 1, 1862, gathered at Turtle Creek in Kerr County to begin a trip to Mexico. They took guns and ammunition but, since they did not see themselves as part of a military expedition, didn't seem to expect any serious military resistance. They were simply fleeing the country to sit out the war in Mexico rather than give into rebel rule.

They made it to the Nueces River on August 9 and set up camp at a spot that no self-respecting military outfit would have chosen. Guard duty was treated as more of a formality than a life-or-death task. Into this apparently relaxed and indefensible camp rode ninety-four Confederate cavalrymen on the morning of August 10. Nineteen Unionists were

The *Treu Der Union* monument.

killed on the battlefield, and nine others later surrendered and were shot. Eight others were killed by Confederate soldiers on October 18 while they tried to cross the Rio Grande into Mexico. Twenty of the men made it to either Mexico or California, and eleven made their way back home.

The soldiers who were killed on the banks of the Nueces were not buried. Not until after the war were their bones gathered and taken back to Comfort to be interred. A monument was erected on August 10, 1866, to commemorate the German Americans and one Hispanic who were killed at the battle and in subsequent actions. The monument was named *Treu Der Union*, or "True to the Union."

The flag that graces the monument has thirty-six stars—the number of states in the Union at the time the monument was dedicated—and is one of only a handful of sites allowed the privilege of permanently flying its flag at half-mast. It is also the only Civil War monument in a former Confederate state dedicated to the Union cause.

JIM BOWIE AND HIS KNIFE

There is a particular scene in one of the many old movies that feature frontiersman Jim Bowie and his knife. In the movie, Bowie follows a meteorite to where it lands and has a blacksmith make him a knife from the meteor.

"This knife has a little bit of heaven in it," the blacksmith tells Bowie. "Or a little bit of hell."

It never happened, just as many of the stories associated with Bowie and the knife named for him never happened. We know for sure that Jim Bowie lived a boisterous and sometimes violent life as a slave trader, fortune hunter and general bon vivant. The legend of the "Lost Bowie Mine" alone is the subject of numerous books and scholarly articles.

We also know that a knife was named for him and used by him and is as connected to him in history as surely as Samuel Colt is associated with the Colt revolver. Bowie's heyday was before Colt's invention, and that is an important part of the Bowie legend.

At a certain time in certain parts of the expanding American frontier, the use of a firearm to settle differences was considered impractical and maybe just a wee bit sissified. The soldiers at San Jacinto are said to have surprised the Mexican army (even more than it was already) when they wielded rifles as billy clubs and finished the job with knives. Reloading and firing was considered way too time consuming for busy revolutionaries on the go. "Use a knife, save ammunition" the saying went.

Jim's brother, Rezin P. Bowie, is generally credited with part of the Bowie design when he cut his hand while trying to kill a wild cow. He asked the plantation blacksmith, Jesse Cliff, to make him a knife that wouldn't slip in the hand. (Rezin Bowie had to draw the first crude design with his left hand because the fingers of his right hand were sliced to the bone.) Cliff then turned out replicas of the knife, which were called Bowies.

The Good, the Bad and the Witty

James Bowie was famous for his knife long before he met his fate at the Alamo. *Library of Congress.*

A good bit of evidence suggests that the real Bowie knife of legend and lore was designed and made in Arkansas when Bowie gave his original knife to an Arkansas blacksmith named Thomas Black and asked him to make a copy of it. Black did so but also designed another knife, the one he had dreamed of making if he could make any knife he wanted. He offered Bowie a choice of the original or his own design, and Bowie quickly chose Black's version. Black's design was long and heavy and was distinguished by an evil little upturn at its tip and a scooped top blade. Though used whenever there was cutting to be done, the Bowie's primary function—to kill—was obvious in its design.

The stories that revolve around Black differ on how much of the design was his and how much was Bowie's or someone else's, but he is always credited with the strength of its blade. Black's knife was made of tempered steel, and it was claimed that he had rediscovered the "Damascus secret," a lost method of tempering Damascus steel that was much in demand during the Crusades.

Legend has it that Bowie decided that he needed a special fighting knife after an adversary began shooting at him during one of the few times in his life when Bowie was unarmed. He borrowed Rezin's knife, the one made by the plantation blacksmith, and used it to persuade the assailant to stop shooting him.

He also used a knife on September 19, 1827, during a fight on a Vidalia, Louisiana sandbar. Apparently, Bowie was part of a pistol duel that got out of hand without honor being settled. Bowie was shot twice and also stabbed during the melee but managed to kill one man and wound another with his knife. From that sandbar, the legend of Jim Bowie and his knife spread far and wide.

Bowie would have been a figure of some note even without his knife. He made a lot of money as a land speculator and also as a slave trader and smuggler. In some accounts, Bowie bought slaves from pirate Jean Laffite for one dollar per pound. Like most of the men who died at the Alamo, Bowie traveled a long and winding road to end up in that little mission in March 1836. He was already gravely ill and fought his last battle from a cot while he and his knife were at the peak of notoriety, but times were changing.

A story related by J. Frank Dobie illustrates that. E.R. Williamson, better known to state history as "Three-Legged Willie," was a judge whose turf included some of the deepest backwoods along the Louisiana-Texas border. He had the honor of presiding over the first session of court in what is now Shelby County. To clue the judge in on how local matters were conducted, a lawyer laid a Bowie knife across the resolution in question and said, "Your honor, this is the law in this country."

Three-Legged Willie responded by placing a six-shooter next to the Bowie knife and said, "This is the Constitution that overrides the law. Sheriff, call the court to order."

The era of the Bowie knife was over and the six-shooter era had begun.

THE NAME RINGS A BELL

Maybe the reason Johnny Ringo's name has stayed in the history books and popular culture for so long is simply because of the name itself— Johnny Ringo. Though newspaper accounts of the day often referred to him as Johnny Ringgold for some reason, his real name was Johnny Ringo. The name has a certain, well, ring to it.

That's probably why so many scriptwriters and western novelists named characters—especially those of the dashing Western outlaw variety—Johnny Ringo. Movies, a TV series or two and even a number one pop song all used the name without much fidelity to the facts. The entertainments might as well have been about Ringo Starr as Johnny Ringo.

John Peters Ringo was born in Indiana, but his family moved to Missouri and then to California before Ringo made his way to Texas. We know that he spent Christmas 1874 in this state because he was arrested in Burnet on Christmas Day of that year for firing a shot across the city square.

Though his reputation today rests mostly on his associations and willingness to take sides in a bloody feud in Tombstone, Arizona, where Wyatt Earp and Doc Holliday were antagonists, he already had a reputation when he arrived in Arizona. The reputation came as a result of his involvement in the Hoodoo War, sometimes called the Mason County War, though its bloody trail extended into several central Texas counties.

Johnny Ringo had a great name but a lousy reputation. *Library of Congress.*

The Hoodoo War started, as so many feuds in those days did, with a dispute over the ownership of certain cattle. The factions split along ethnic lines and pitted recent German settlers against American-born men in neighboring counties. Many of the German settlers had supported the North during the Civil War, which bred resentment and hostility in the area.

Well into the hostilities of the Hoodoo War, Ringo and a man named Bill Williams visited a man named Jim Cheyney, who lived along Comanche Creek in Mason County. Cheyney didn't know he was a marked man, so he invited Ringo and Williams to have breakfast with him. After breakfast, while Cheyney was washing his face, Williams and Ringo shot and killed him.

The pair then rode to Mason, where they approached David Doole's store and demanded that Doole come outside, presumably so they could shoot him, too. Doole wisely declined. Ringo and Williams moseyed on over to the Lace Bridges Hotel, where they engaged in some Old West trash talk about "some fresh meat up on the creek" and then they rode away.

Ringo and another participant in the Hoodoo War, Scott Cooley, were arrested in December 1875, possibly in connection with the old charge against Ringo for his Christmas Day gunplay the year before. Ringo and Cooley were shuttled back and forth between Austin and Burnet, attracting much attention along the way, before being taken to the jail in Lampasas to await trial.

Allies of the pair determined that they should be removed from the jail as quickly as possible, mob violence being what it was in those days. Four men showed up in Lampasas on the night of April 30, captured the jail guard and tied him to a fence. They tried to cut a hole in the jail but failed. They took the jailer down the road a few miles toward San Saba and released him unharmed.

Four days later, they tried again. This time they secured the keys to the jail at gunpoint, released Cooley and Ringo without a lot of trouble and rode back to Joe Olney's ranch in Llano County, where Ringo was staying.

Ringo was arrested again the next year for the Cheyney killing. He spent most of 1876 and 1877 in jail awaiting trial before the case was dismissed. He settled in Loyal Valley for a time, and records indicate that he was elected constable in that community but served little if any time in that capacity.

By 1879, he was in Arizona, where he shot a man named Louis Hancock for ordering beer when Ringo had specifically told him to order whiskey. In Tombstone, Johnny Ringo was known as "King of the Cowboys" in reference to his standing among the group that opposed Wyatt Earp, his brothers and Doc Holliday in that town.

In the 1993 movie *Tombstone*, Ringo is killed by Doc Holliday in a gunfight but not before Ringo sprouts off some Latin phrases at him. Though there is a great deal of disagreement over exactly how Ringo ended up with a bullet in his head—Holliday and Earp are sometimes pointed to as the cause—most sources hold with the "official" version: the last person Johnny Ringo killed was himself.

JACOB BRODBECK TAKES FLIGHT

To a long list of Texas boasts, we can possibly add one more: the first manned flight. While the Johnny-come-lately Wright brothers have claimed the distinction in our history books, it's possible that a German immigrant who settled in Luckenbach, Jacob Friedrich Brodbeck, beat the Wright brothers to the punch by some thirty-eight years.

Of course, if we're talking about a "successful" manned flight, well, that's another matter, but aviators have always said that any landing you walk away from is a good landing. By that definition, Brodbeck's flight was a success.

Jacob Brodbeck was born in Germany in 1821 and arrived in Texas in 1847. He served as the surveyor for Gillespie County and also worked as the district school supervisor and as a county commissioner. He was a smart guy. In Germany, he invented a self-winding clock but is said to have been mighty insulted when a German king offered him the equivalent of one cow for his invention. Brodbeck left the country in a huff and headed for America, where he kept tinkering with things in between his various jobs.

In Texas, Brodbeck designed an ice-making machine. His wife, Maria, enjoyed the luxury of a powered washing machine in the 1860s; the washer was designed by her husband using the power takeoff from a

Jacob Brodbeck built an airplane before anybody knew what to call it.

windmill. Brodbeck's grandest project, one that he worked on for twenty years, was what he called an "air-ship." The word "airplane" didn't exist yet, nor did its precursor, "aero plane." Ditto the internal combustion engine. Air-ship it was.

Brodbeck's air-ship had a rudder, wings and a propeller powered by coiled springs. His first design was basically a glider that could be launched from a ramp and fly for three or four minutes before gently descending earthward. That was a fine amusement, but Brodbeck had loftier ambitions; he wanted an air-ship that could take you places. To increase the flight time, Brodbeck designed two interdependent clock motors for his airship. The design called for one motor to rewind the other. When one motor became unwound, the second motor would be engaged to rewind the first one. When that motor unwound, the first motor would be engaged again to rewind the other motor.

Details of his first and only flight are sketchy at best—and contradictory. Some accounts have it taking place in a field about three miles west of Luckenbach, but it might have happened at San Pedro Park in San Antonio, where a bust of Brodbeck is displayed. Most accounts suggest that the flight took place in 1865, but others say it didn't happen until 1868.

As a theory, Brodbeck's concept of interdependent clock motors was a flawless bit of genius. In practice, the flight came to a sudden halt when the spring tension of the first motor became equal to the spring tension in the second motor. As a result, both motors became unwound after attaining a height of about twelve feet and a distance of about one hundred feet; the whole contraption came tumbling to the ground.

Brodbeck crawled from the wreckage, unhurt and undeterred. He asked his investors to finance a second attempt, but they had seen enough; they refused to put any more money into Brodbeck's air-ship.

Still determined to create a machine that could transport people through the air, Brodbeck embarked on a fundraising tour of the United States to secure funds for a second attempt. During the tour, his papers detailing the new and improved design for his airship were either lost or stolen. Audiences and would-be investors remained skeptical.

Finally, Brodbeck returned to his ranch near Luckenbach, where he lived out his remaining years. He lived until 1910, long enough to hear of the Wright brothers' success at Kitty Hawk. The success of the Wright brothers' flying machine created some interest in Brodbeck's invention, but no drawings or blueprints of his air-ship survived.

Texas would go on to have a rich aviation history, but Brodbeck's contributions have endured mostly as a footnote. In 1985, at Fort Sam Houston (the birthplace of military aviation in this country), air force historians brought together several of Brodbeck's descendants to recognize his contribution to manned flight.

The man deserved at least that much. History has to give Brodbeck credit for trying to invent a flying machine at a time when most people believed that heavier-than-air flight was impossible. Just because he couldn't disprove that notion didn't mean that it wasn't true.

ALEX SWEET AND HIS SIFTINGS

In terms of popularity and a reputation for being a real Texas wiseguy, Alex Sweet could be called the Kinky Friedman of his day. Sweet's day was roughly the last half of the nineteenth century. When Texas was wild and woolly, Alex Sweet was there to make fun of it all.

Sweet knew that Texans made fun of the very notions that both formed the Texas mythology and kept settlers away in droves. He described the "typical" Texan, a blue norther, the vexations of a red ant sting, the high comedy of stagecoach robberies and the "official" accounts of Indian battles in ways that are still funny today. In a piece titled "That Typical Texan," written in the 1870s, he notes that people in the North had in their minds a fixed image of the typical Texan: "The typical Texan is a large-sized Jabberwock, a hairy kind of gorilla, who is supposed to reside on a horse…He is expected to carry four of five revolvers on his belt, as if he were a sort of perambulating gunrack…The only time the typical Texan is supposed to be peaceable is after he has killed all his friends, and can find no fresh materials to practice on."

At the same time, Sweet points out that stagecoach robberies in west Texas had become so common that passengers "complained to the stage companies if they came through unmolested." Sweet's point was that many of the robberies would not have occurred if even one of the passengers were a typical Texan. "The typical Texan acted more in accordance with the New Testament, where it requires the plundered party, who has been robbed of his coat, to pull off his pants, and tender them to the needy highwayman," he wrote.

Sweet, who grew up in San Antonio, moved to Austin in 1881 and, with partner John Armoy Knox, began publishing an eight-page weekly humor magazine called *Texas Siftings*. The magazine quickly reached a circulation of fifty thousand and expanded to three times that number by the late 1880s. The *New York Post* hailed Sweet as "second to no living writer in freshness, originality, sparkling wit and refined humor."

In writing about Mexico's pursuit of Mescalero Apaches into Texas, Sweet noticed that dispatches of the pursuit seemed to center on the same band of Apaches that the Mexicans apparently defeated on several different occasions. "They have captured the same band of hostile Indians, Mescaleros, four successive times, and each time they make out of it a fresh crowd," he noted. He noted that of the eighty-five Indians in the original band captured by a Colonel Ortiz, five were killed trying to escape. As similar reports were filed, Sweet did the math:

> *By the time the Indians reach the City of Mexico they* [the Mexicans] *will have taken prisoners, if this bad luck is kept up, 879,483,214,812 Mescaleros out of the 81 that started out.*
>
> *If the five Indians that have been killed four times in traveling 50 miles continue to resist arrest they will have to leave a graveyard, for there will have fallen in the conflict 1,897,658 Indians out of the original five who were shot by Col. Ortiz only two months ago. This is a dreadful mortality.*

While wildly popular in his day, Sweet is rarely mentioned today in reviews of American or even Texas literature or humor. That his writing is available at all is largely due to the efforts of Virginia Eisenhour, who edited the best of Sweet's work and compiled it in the 1986 University of Texas Press book *Alex Sweet's Texas: The Lighter Side of Lone Star History*.

The collection contains sixty-three of Sweet's "siftings," including one that parodied the "personal" ads of the day. Sweet made up his own list of eligible bachelors, including Colonel Horace B. Yammer, who is "very regular in his habits—he is always drunk before 10 o'clock in the morning."

He also turned his attention to Texas critters, such as the longhorn cow that had been branded so many times "she looks as if a sum in algebra had broken out all over her," along with horned lizards, red ants, mosquitoes and roadrunners.

Most of the subjects in the book have been treated by generations of writers who followed Sweet, but few delivered the goods with a slight elbow to the ribs like Sweet did. He's proof that Texans have never much cared if people from other places make fun of us, because we have always done that better than they do anyway.

O. Henry in Texas

While he was not born here, he didn't die here and many of his best-known stories are not set here, William S. Porter, better known to generations of readers as O. Henry, was as much a Texan as he was anything else. If he could have stayed out of trouble here, he probably wouldn't have left the state at all. Fleeing the authorities was a time-honored frontier tradition in Texas, and Porter carried on that tradition.

Porter was born and grew up in North Carolina, where he appeared to be settling into the life of a drugstore clerk until he read an advertisement for Texas as a state "growing faster than the sideburns of a thirty-year old." He was a somewhat sickly young man with a persistent cough; the clean air and wide open spaces of Texas sounded like a new lease on life. As the saying goes, he wasn't born in Texas but got here as fast as he could.

Once he got to Texas, Porter might have been one of many over the years who have groused, "There's a lot of things they didn't tell me when I signed on with this outfit." Working on a ranch in LaSalle County included getting up before sunrise to feed cattle. If he wanted to go town, he had to ride a horse, and once he got to town, there wasn't much more entertainment than there was back at the ranch.

Though his stint on the ranch lasted only a couple of years, he availed himself of the ranch family's well-stocked library, and he wrote some of his first short stories at the ranch. Later, ranch and rural Texas life, along with the state's rich trove of legends and lore, informed many of his best-known short stories.

When the ranch was sold, Porter moved to Austin and worked in a cigar store and in the general land office. By all accounts, Porter enjoyed

This is the house in Austin, now a museum, in which writer O. Henry lived before he was sentenced to prison.

himself immensely in Austin. He was a regular at most of the saloon's in town and was in demand as a drinking companion because he was an agreeable drunk who preferred telling wild stories to fighting while under the influence. He married and went to work for the First National Bank in Austin as a teller despite having no experience and, apparently, no talent for the job.

To supplement his income and his interest, he published his own weekly newspaper, the *Rolling Stone*. The paper, consisting mostly of Porter's drawings and satirical prose sketches, did well at first but faltered quickly and went out of business. Porter had heard many of the "lost treasure" stories that abounded in Texas, and he followed one such tale to Shoal Creek in Austin, but the treasure he sought remained lost and Porter remained broke.

The career as a bank teller came to a screeching halt in 1894 when a bank examiner couldn't make heads or tails of Porter's till—other than the fact that there wasn't as much money in it as there was supposed to be. He was accused of embezzlement and was defended by his co-workers, but the bank pursued charges. His father-in-law negotiated a settlement, and Porter went to work writing a column for the *Houston Daily Post* that proved promising, but troubles back at the bank escalated.

Porter was an easy scapegoat when the bank's books were found to be riddled with shortages and discrepancies. He didn't know enough about the banking business to defend himself, and he couldn't afford a lawyer. Considering all his options, he hopped a steamer to Honduras.

Porter adapted well to island life. He drank freely and shared stories with a fugitive bank robber he befriended. He wrote to his wife, Athol, asking her to join him in his island paradise but found out that she was ill and not expected to live much longer.

Resigning himself to his own fate, he returned to Austin to be with Athol. He was arrested and convicted of stealing two checks from the bank, but charges of embezzling the larger amounts were dropped. He was sentenced to five years in the federal penitentiary at Columbus, Ohio. There he worked in the prison pharmacy and wrote a lot of short stories, which were by now being published by national magazines. The publishing world of New York City and literary immortality were waiting on him when he was released from prison.

Porter first began using the pseudonym O. Henry in Austin. He adopted it again in New York, possibly to keep from being traced back to that convicted embezzler. He published more than three hundred stories under that name. The stories were collected into nine best-selling volumes during his lifetime and many more in subsequent years.

Many of the Texas stories can be found in the 1907 collection *The Heart of the West*. He also created the character the Cisco Kid, which was the basis of the 1950s television series of the same name. The country's most prestigious short story award is named in his honor, and his work is still in print and still widely read.

Part III

FROM DINOSAURS TO POLO

IN PRAISE OF THE UNAPPRECIATED MULE

Let's talk about mules. Horses are quick to grab Texas history's glamour and glory, leaving little attention for their homelier, obstinate cousin. Can you imagine the Lone Ranger charging to the rescue on a mule? While acknowledging the mule's notable lack of charisma, old-timers are quick to point out that the horse/donkey half-breed is a forgotten hero.

"A lot of people never think about it, but mules made the United States," says Clements W. "Speedy" Duncan in the book *Harder Than Hardscrabble*, an oral history about growing up on the lands now occupied by Fort Hood. "They [mules] built all the railroads, and they did all the farming, and they pulled them wagon trains across the country. They don't get their just credit, mules don't. The cotton-picking old mule is the most unappreciated thing that ever happened to this country."

Christopher Columbus appreciated mules enough to take some on a 1493 voyage to what is now Haiti. George Washington bred horses but started the mule industry in this country when the king of Spain gave him a mule as a gift. Washington felt that horses "ate too much, worked too little, and died too young" to be of much use on the farm.

To early Texas farmers, buying mules was as important as buying a car or truck is today, but mules did not come with a 100,000-mile warranty or cash-back rebates. Texas led the country for a few years in

The much-maligned mule was an important part of early rural life. *Library of Congress.*

the production of mules—well over a million of them in 1926, about the time that newfangled internal combustion engine really started catching on.

Willie Huber of Belfalls, ninety-six when I interviewed him a few years ago, recalled that his first, most important, purchase when he started farming for himself seven decades ago was a team of mules. He found four for sale at a farm about ten miles west of Gatesville and went to have a look. He liked what he saw in three of the mules, but he had his doubts about the fourth one. He was right about the first three. Unfortunately, he was right about the fourth one, too.

"That fourth mule wasn't no count," he ruefully admitted some seventy years later.

In *Harder than Hardscrabble*, T.A. Wilhite described the traits he looked for back in his mule trading days. "You wanted them to have muscle, and you wanted them to have the right kind of disposition," he said. "You might get scalped many times 'til you learned what to look for."

The U.S. Army recognized the value of mules early on. Mules served in every American conflict between 1820 and 1945. They were essential to both the North and the South in the Civil War. A thousand marching soldiers required at least twenty-five wagons to carry supplies and haul heavy artillery from one battle site to another, and mules pulled most of those wagons. When told that Confederate soldiers had captured forty mules and a Union general, Abraham Lincoln reportedly responded, "I'm sorry to lose those mules."

In *Shavetails and Bell Sharps: History of the U.S. Army Mule*, author Emmett M. Essin writes that the army found mules to be stronger and more agile than either a horse or a donkey, able to carry heavier loads longer distances over more difficult terrain. "Mules were also sensitive, intelligent animals, more so than their parent stock. They quickly recognized approaching danger and knew by instinct how to avoid it," he wrote. On the battle lines, however, mules often became conscientious objectors, recognizing the high probability of death the battlefield presented. Maybe that's why you never saw a lot of mules charging into battle.

Gradually, tractors replaced mules on the farm, leaving them with nothing more than a reputation for being stubborn. But a few places still pay homage to the mule's contribution. Texas is one of those places. The National Mule Memorial is in—where else?—Muleshoe, and it was financed with private donations, including twenty-five cents from a mule driver in Uzbekistan. The mule gets its just credit in Muleshoe.

The mule is also recognized in the Coryell County town of Topsey, which is named for an early farmer's favorite mule. Mule Ear Peaks, in the Chisos Mountains of west Texas, is an easily recognizable and aptly named geographic feature. Still, even with its own monument, even with towns and landmarks named in its honor, the mule remains the Rodney Dangerfield of the animal world, getting no respect. To make matters worse, it is often confused with other equine critters, like donkeys.

Remember: a donkey is just a donkey; a mule is a cross between a horse and a donkey, usually a male donkey and a female horse, but not necessarily. A cross between a male horse and a female donkey is called a hinny.

Just don't be a jackass and call a mule a donkey. Mules deserve a little more respect than that.

CAMELS FOR TEXAS

If Jefferson Davis and others could have had their way, camels might have become as much a symbol of Texas ingenuity and grit as the longhorn or the mustang. Mules, oxen and other beasts of burden might have found themselves ignominiously unemployed when it came to time to cross American deserts and mountains. Rodeos and horse tracks would look a lot different, and cowboys would have a whole different set of skills. It could have happened.

That it didn't work out quite that way isn't wholly the fault of the camels. They proved more than adequate for the tasks assigned them but Davis, Robert E. Lee (who was charged with protecting the camels for a time when he was stationed in Texas) and indeed the entire country was forced to take on other considerations, mainly a little episode in our history known as the American Civil War. As much as anything, politics doomed the camel experiment in Texas.

If Jefferson Davis could have had his way, camels would have become a part of the Texas landscape. Harper's Weekly *Postcard Collection.*

Davis, a U.S. senator who would later serve as the U.S. secretary of war, had long supported the annexation of Texas, but transportation in the rougher portions of the state, especially west Texas, was problematic. Accepting the commonly held notion that most of the western United States was a Great American Desert, Davis thought that camels might be the solution.

As secretary of war, Davis's first annual report to President Franklin Pierce included some lobbying on behalf of the humble and hardworking dromedary. "Napoleon when in Egypt used with marked success the dromedary in subduing the Arabs whose habits and country were very similar to those of the mounted Indians of our Western plains," Davis wrote. "France is about to adopt the dromedary in Algeria. For like military purposes, for expresses and for reconnaissance, it is believed that the dromedary will fill a want now seriously felt in our military service." In 1857, Davis helped add $30,000 to the appropriation bill for the "purchase of camels and the importation of dromedaries, to be employed for military purposes."

And so it came to pass that thirty-two camels—mostly single-humped Arabian dromedaries along with a two-humped Bactrian and hybrids of the two (plus one calf born at sea)—arrived at the historic but now defunct port city of Indianola in the spring of 1857. Major H.C. Wayne, who bought the camels during a trafficking foray up and down the North African coast, brought them to Texas, eventually settling at Camp Verde in the Hill Country near present-day Kerrville. From that base of operations, those camels, along with a second group from Egypt, went to work with the same accepting nonchalance for which they are known.

Wayne's first test was an expedition sending six camels from Camp Verde to San Antonio; the camels passed with flying colors. "From this trial it will be seen that the six camels transported over the same ground and distance the weights of two six mule wagons, and gained on them 42½ hours in time," Wayne reported. Other reports confirmed the fact that camels were up to about any task assigned them. Skeptics might have been persuaded by a trip to the Big Bend region of Texas, a rugged and arid land that had defeated previous expeditions.

For the camels, the trip was pretty much a walk in the park. The camels at one point traveled more than one hundred miles in four days without water, which allowed the human members of the expedition to save their water without a need to share it with horses or mules, as would have been the case in a traditional trip to those parts. The group eventually found water, and it was reported that the camels "arrived at the water in good condition and showed no evidence of unusual distress."

In response to complaints from pioneers who found westbound travel more than a little perilous, not to mention downright difficult, Lieutenant Edward Beale was instructed to take a caravan from Texas to California. Like Wayne and others, Beale saw a lot to like in the camels. He wrote, "They are the most docile, patient and easily managed creatures in the world and infinitely more workable than mules." Not all the camels made it back to Texas from California. A few stayed in the Golden State and were seen there as late as the 1890, wandering aimlessly about the deserts in a typically laid-back California attitude.

The Great Camel Experiment died from neglect, as did the camels from a couple of other subsequent shipments of camels to the state. As hostilities between the North and South escalated, Jefferson Davis became president of the Confederacy. Robert E. Lee refused to fight against his home state and also joined the Confederacy. U.S. officials were quick to wash their hands of any enterprise that had Davis's fingerprints on it, and Confederate troops who took over Camp Verde during the Civil War let a lot of the animals escape into the hills, where they scared witless many an unsuspecting traveler or newcomer. Comanches called them "goats of the devil."

While it may be surmised that Texas and the United States missed a good opportunity when it let the camel experiment die, that's probably not the case. We can only imagine what kind of havoc camels would have wrought on native vegetation. While reports from military officers were laudatory, not everyone was so fond of the camels. They smelled bad and could be extremely foul-tempered. Camels also have an annoying habit of vomiting or spitting on people who displease them. Even the most stubborn of mules won't resort to pukery.

Horses hate camels, too. "The chief objection to using camels as beasts of burden in Texas is that horses usually run away at the sight of them," one observer wrote. "This is bad for the horse and worse for the pilot of the camel if the owners of the horses should have his pistol with him."

Using camels in the American deserts and mountains was an idea whose time came, and we can be glad for that because it added a colorful chapter to our history, but we can be just as glad that the idea passed. It's hard to imagine the Seventh Cavalry riding to the rescue on a bunch of camels.

First in War, First in Polo

One of the few recreations available to settlers on the Texas frontier was horse races. Early settlers brought their fondness of short-distance pony races with them from places like Tennessee and Missouri, and that form of sport became popular and led to the development of a lot of fast Texas quarter horses. Texans liked horse races, which led breeders to make them even faster by improving the strain with the best pony-built mares in the country.

By the time eastern markets like Boston, Philadelphia and New York sought to purchase horses bred for the sport of polo, Texas breeders found that they had been breeding such a horse all along. The U.S. Cavalry knew this long before the East Coast polo clubs. The 1904 *Texas Almanac* noted that "while no systematic attempt has been made to breed polo ponies, conditions of climate and pasturage, combined with peculiarities of breed, have tended to produce an appreciable number of these highly-prized and fleet-footed accessories to the rich man's game. By far, the largest number, especially of the higher class of ponies, come from Texas."

George Miller, an Austin horse trader, knew early on that Texas horses would perform as well on the polo field as the battlefield. Most of the horses purchased for the East Coast polo clubs were from Texas, and Miller sold a good many of those horses. Dennis Antolik, president of the Austin Polo Club, said that polo and Texas quarter horses were a perfect fit.

"The U.S. Cavalry was already buying a lot of Texas horses, and they used a lot of them for polo because most if not all the military schools of the day had polo teams, and the Texas horses were perfect for the sport," Antolik said. "George Patton was an avid polo player, and so was Winston Churchill. They both learned to play in the military. All the major military schools had polo teams, and a lot of the officers continued with the sport the rest of their lives."

Horses bred in Texas turned out to be perfect for the sport of polo. *Library of Congress.*

Antolik said that it's possible that the first American polo matches, unofficial as they may have been, were played in Texas because a large number of wandering or dispossessed lords and dukes and counts ended up owning vast parcels of Texas land. Some of them drifted or were banished here and no doubt brought the sport with them. "That was the social class that played polo in England, so it's pretty safe to assume that they figured out a way to play it when they got here," Antolik said.

By the early part of the twentieth century, breeders could sell a horse to the cavalry for $165 or sell it for $300 as a polo pony. That inspired some cowboys to start swinging mallets at objects on the ground while astride a horse so they could say they had trained that horse for polo. The "Golden Age" of polo in America was the 1920s, when Cecil Smith and other Texas players, like Rube Williams, were at their peak. Another Texan, Fred Roe, earned a silver medal in polo at the 1924 Olympics.

The Austin Polo Club was formed in 1925, not long after the founding of the San Antonio Polo Club. A club was formed about the same time in Houston. The U.S. Polo Association lists twenty-eight polo clubs in the state, including club teams at several universities. The Texas A&M University Polo Club has won nine national championships since 1994. An annual event on the Lazy 3 Ranch near Albany known as "Polo on the Prairie" has raised more than $3 million for cancer research and patient care programs of the M.D. Anderson Cancer Center.

Polo gets most of its publicity these days not from superstars of the sport like Cecil Smith but superstars from other arenas, including actor Tommy Lee Jones, who rides for the San Saba Club, and country music superstar George Strait. The wider world may think that they are bucking tradition by playing polo in a state forged from a rugged frontier, but Texas horse breeders have known all along that this was the real birthplace of polo in this country.

COWBOY KING OF POLO

In addition to riding, roping and branding, some Texas cowboys turned out to be pretty good polo players. One of them, Cecil Smith, became the best polo player of all time, a Michael Jordan or Babe Ruth of the sport. Smith was from Oxford—Texas, that is, in Llano County—where he learned to ride by the age of three and was a champion youth roper. He went to work for horse trader George Miller and taught himself the fundamentals of polo by fashioning a polo mallet out of a broom handle and hitting rocks and tin cans.

Miller recalled what those days were like in a 1977 *Sports Illustrated* story about Smith. "It was about like learning to play baseball in a railroad switchyard," he said. "Cecil hit that ball a wallop and it went about a mile. I didn't say anything, but I thought about it when I got back to my place."

Cecil Smith was introduced to his life's calling when Miller and Rube Williams showed up at the Moss Ranch in Llano County, where Smith was working with a couple of horses they had bought as prospective polo ponies. Miller provided Smith with a mallet and some balls, and Smith learned how to play on the rocky hillsides of Llano County.

"They started stick-and-balling some horses, and they asked me to stick-and-ball some, which I did, and that's how I got started," Smith

Cecil Smith, in the dark shirt at the back of the photo, in action at the 1933 "World Series" of polo in Lake Forest, Illinois. Chicago History Museum, from the *Chicago Daily News* negative collection.

recounted. "It was a lot of fun. I had roped calves quite a bit before I ever swung a mallet, and roping calves and hitting a polo ball are quite a bit alike; it's a matter of timing."

When Smith took up the sport, polo had been described as "the smallest, wealthiest, most exclusive group ever to represent the U.S. in international sport." Cecil Smith was a lot of things, but "wealthy" was not one of them. The polo establishment didn't quite know what to make of this Texas ranch hand who managed to make the task of swinging a mallet with exquisite timing and accuracy while astride a galloping quarter horse look almost easy.

Smith's mastery of the game was recognized nationally in 1933 in a much-publicized polo match between the East and the West—basically the elite East Coast players, including superstar Tommy Hitchcock, against a bunch of players described, somewhat disparagingly, as cowboys. The general feeling was that the cowboys didn't stand a chance.

In that match, played in August 1933 at the Onwentsia Club in Lake Forest, Smith scored six goals despite being knocked unconscious for twenty-three minutes in a stunning 15–11 victory for the West. Brigadier General Sam Marshall, the Army's World War II historian and a polo enthusiast, called it "the most dramatic upset in a generation...Smith outthought Hitchcock, out rode him and outhit him by a wide margin," he wrote.

Polo players are ranked on a theoretical value of "goals" with ten being just about perfect. Very few players ever achieve such rarified status, but Smith held the ranking for twenty-five consecutive years, the longest streak of its kind in polo history. Smith settled in Llano for several years when his polo playing days were done and continued to raise horses for the rest of his life. He was a first-ballot selection to the Polo Hall of Fame in 1990. He played his last polo game at age eighty-three and last rode when he was ninety-two. He died in Boerne in 1999 at the age of ninety-four.

Smith's citation in the Polo Hall of Fame reads in part: "Cecil Smith was endowed with unquestionable talents both as a horseman and polo player. With determination and fortitude he developed his abilities to perfection. Over the years, he played on more fields with more players than perhaps anyone in polo. He has always been and still is the inspirational leader of the game."

Batty in Texas

Geologically, the Texas Hill Country is where the West begins. Coming east across the coastal plain and the Blackland Prairie, the flatland gives way at Austin to wooded hills bisected by the Colorado River and its tributaries running west to east across the craggy hills. The thin soils lying atop limestone provide the perfect ingredients for flash floods, which have plagued the region for millennia. Here and there in the Hill Country, the land is marked by giant boulders and batholiths, the biggest and most famous being Enchanted Rock. Juniper, commonly called cedar, along with mesquite, oaks and cacti give the land character and color. There are also thousands of caves, many of them quite large, and some have evolved into tourist attractions. Others are still the domain of millions of Mexican freetail bats that make the caves their home from spring until late fall every year.

Bats have been coming to the Texas Hill Country for millions of years, inspiring one man to use them to combat disease and another to turn them into bombs. *Leroy Williamson.*

The bats love Texas for the same reason a lot of people do: geography and climate. Bats love caves, and the state has some three thousand caves and sinkholes, though most of the bat colonies are concentrated in about two dozen of those caves. Bracken Cave near Fredericksburg has a thriving metropolis of twenty million bats, the largest-known bat colony in the world. Those twenty million bats can eat two hundred tons of insects in a single night, including mosquitoes and agricultural pests that plague cotton and corn crops.

While taking sensible precautions in regards to bats as carriers of rabies, we have asked our bats to wipe out other diseases. We have even enlisted bats in the war effort. Results of these experiments have been mixed.

Early in the twentieth century, Dr. Charles Campbell, a San Antonio physician, built a "municipal bat roost" as part of an effort to fight malaria, which killed millions of people worldwide each year. Dr. Campbell saw the ravages of the disease in some his own patients and wondered if bats could be colonized like bees in bat towers to prosper and multiply and end the ravages of malaria once and for all.

Bats turned out to be pickier about where they lived than Dr. Campbell first imagined; they stayed away from his first bat towers in droves. Giving the matter closer observation, he decided to try again, this time closer to water. A bat tower he built in 1911 near swampy Mitchell's Lake a few miles south of San Antonio proved the first glimmer of hope. Mitchell's Lake was notorious for its hordes of mosquitoes and no wonder: this was where San Antonio's sewage flowed, creating perfect breeding grounds for mosquitoes. Tenant farmers in the area were so bedeviled by the swarms of mosquitoes that they often were forced to leave their fields untended and the livestock in sorry condition. Dr. Campbell later wrote that of eighty-seven people he examined near Mitchell's Lake in 1911, seventy-eight suffered from malaria.

The bat tower at Mitchell's Lake brought a few bats the first year and more bats the next year but a veritable horde the following year. Where it once took him five minutes to watch the bats spiral from the tower each summer evening, it soon took two hours. People came and watched the spectacle, much as the bat roost under the Congress Avenue Bridge today attracts visitors every evening when the bats are in town.

Within four years, farmers near Mitchell's Lake reported that they could now work their fields without being attacked by dense clouds of bloodsucking mosquitoes. Malaria all but disappeared from the area.

Dr. Campbell's efforts brought him a Nobel Peace Prize nomination in 1919, but the bat towers soon faded from public consciousness and the landscape. There may be a handful of the original towers left here and there, but most have given way to the ravages of time and progress. A site on private property west of Sisterdale in Kendall County is believed to be the only one still in existence.

In a 1989 article for the Bat Conservation International magazine, editor Mari Murphy noted that the disappearance of malaria about the time of Dr. Mitchell's bat towers was well documented, but the extent to which the roosts could be credited was not scientifically studied and thus open to question. "The success of Dr. Campbell's experiments can no longer be tested, since most of his bat roosts and the original mosquito breeding conditions are now gone," she wrote.

While Dr. Campbell's bat towers are viewed today as an idea that just might have worked—we can't say for sure—an idea hatched in top secrecy during World War II leaves no room for such ambiguity.

Not long after the Japanese bombing of Pearl Harbor, the U.S. government put an oddball cast of characters to work researching how bats might be turned into small incendiary bombs and dropped on Japan. Really. The research was carried out in unlikely places like Bandera, Carlsbad, New Mexico and California. It cost about $2 million and involved a lot of risky behavior in caves, recruiting these unlikely flying mammals into the war effort.

The plan concocted by the researchers involved refrigerating the bats into hibernation and then equipping them with tiny parcels of napalm and little bitty parachutes and dropping them on Japanese cities, which would burn to the ground when the bats flew into the nearest buildings. That was the plan.

Details of the unlikely project, from batty conception to fiery conclusion, is chronicled by the youngest member of the team, Jack Couffer, in his book *Bat Bomb: World War II's Other Secret Weapon*, published by the University of Texas Press in 1992.

As it turned out, the bats couldn't be whisked into hibernation and snapped out of it on any kind of convenient or reliable schedule. The parachutes were too small. The napalm bombs were too big. When the bat bombs were tossed from airplanes some of the bats hit the ground without ever waking up while others ended up with broken wings. A few lucky ones survived the free fall and flew off, just as expected, into the nearest buildings, which turned out to be the airport hangars at a brand new military airfield. The hangars burned to the ground, a general's automobile was incinerated and that was that.

The military dropped the bat bomb project but proceeded with another plan that showed promise, something called an atomic bomb.

THE STRANGE SAGA OF TOM SLICK

First, there was the name. Tom Slick. It sounds daring and adventurous, like Clutch Cargo, Johnny Quest or Indiana Jones. That trio of heroes are each fictional, but Tom Slick lived in the real world, even if he spent a lot of time and money looking for creatures that many people believed to be unreal.

Tom Slick made a name for himself in Texas and in the wider world as millionaire oilman, rancher, businessman and philanthropist. His father,

From Dinosaurs to Polo

Thomas Baker Slick Sr., was a famous and wildly successful wildcatter known as "Lucky Tom" who died young, at age forty-six, and left his children $15 million.

After his mother remarried, Slick's stepfather was kidnapped. Maybe as a result of that experience and his wealth, Tom Slick Jr. would become a private man who shunned the spotlight. He settled in San Antonio with his millions, an insatiable and sometimes unconventional curiosity and a strong desire to do great things without drawing a lot of attention. That wasn't always possible. Spending millions of dollars to look for creatures that science has never acknowledged does tend to draw attention. Slick's biographer, Loren Coleman, refers to Slick as "Texas' forgotten millionaire."

In addition to his oil and ranching business and contributions to research science, Slick also made a name for himself as a cryptozoologist—one who searches for animals that science has never officially acknowledged. Think the Loch Ness monster and then think of the yeti, Sasquatch or Bigfoot, and you get the idea.

Slick drew some national attention when he funded and participated in expeditions to the Himalayas in the 1950s in search of the yeti, the original abominable snowman. Slick and his teams never found anything that science could hang its hat on and say, "By golly, I think we have discovered a new creature! A yeti!" But they unearthed some tantalizing clues that, as the years passed, have unfortunately been lost. While Slick and his team were pounding the Himalayas for proof of the yeti's existence, there was a considerable if not widespread belief that yetis existed but in such harsh and remote environments that finding one, even its remains, was almost impossible.

Yeti fever peaked in the late 1950s and then plunged when famed mountaineer Sir Edmund Hillary effectively put an end to the public's fascination with any notion of an abominable snowman. Hillary, the first man credited with climbing Mount Everest, signed on with a TV crew featuring Marlin Perkins of *Wild Kingdom* fame and went to the Himalayas in sort of a made-for-TV search for the yeti. In lieu of actually spotting one, Hillary tracked down fakes and misrepresentations and used them to debunk the whole notion of a yeti.

Annoyed but undeterred, Slick turned his attentions to another reported man-ape creature, this one said to be living deep in the woods of the Pacific Northwest: Sasquatch, often referred to as Bigfoot.

That we know anything at all about Tom Slick's search for the yeti and Bigfoot is due almost entirely to Coleman's efforts. A cryptozoologist himself, Coleman spent the better part of thirty years researching Tom Slick's life, particularly as it related to his contributions to cryptozoology. The result was his 1989 book *Tom Slick and the Search for the Yeti.*

Coleman wrote in the introduction to his book: "This man would throw his fortune behind a serious search for the mysterious creatures. Who was this man? He was a handsome, lean, prematurely white-haired man, soft spoken, with a slight Southern drawl. Tom Slick was his name, more fictional-sounding than real. And in many ways, Tom Slick's life was the stuff legends are made of…Tom Slick was given many names during his short, event-filled life. But today, hardly anyone remembers him. And that's a shame."

Like his father, Slick died when he was forty-six. A plane he was riding in exploded over Montana in 1962. Had he lived, Tom Slick might have hooked up with or even founded the Texas Bigfoot Research Conservancy, which carries on Slick's interests in Texas. The Texas Bigfoot is believed to be a southern cousin of the Pacific Northwest's Sasquatch. Of the one hundred or so sightings reported on the center's website, the center deems about seventy-five of those sightings as legitimate in the way that sightings of unidentified flying objects are legitimate; both remain unidentified. Persistent reports of a Sasquatch-like creature living along the Sulphur River, just across the state line in Arkansas, inspired the movie *Legend of Boggy Creek.*

The modern-day Texas Bigfoots (Bigfeet?) go by many names, some of which sound like high-end fishing lures: Night Screamer, Hawley Him, Haskell Rascal, Wooly Bugger and Caddo Critter. The people at the Texas Bigfoot Research Conservancy believe that the sightings indicate a primate, albeit an elusive one for which no remains have ever been positively identified. Recent sightings have occurred in the Sam Houston National Forest, near the San Jacinto River. We might say that all of this started with Tom Slick, but to call him Texas's first cryptozoologist we would have to dismiss the Comanches, Tonkawas and other Texas tribes who believed strongly in a man-ape creature in the same way that they believed in, say, bears.

The Hill Country has had a few sightings, too. One came in 1902 in a cedar chopper community called Panther Path in Travis County. A group of young people were fishing and hunting in the area above the old McDonald Dam when a hairy, eight-foot-tall man confronted the young sportsmen with a large club, the better to pulverize them. Bigfoot let loose a bloodcurdling scream and advanced in what can only be described as a menacing manner toward the terrified young people. They ran for the wagons and barely made it. Bigfoot followed them for a while before giving up and disappearing into legend and lore. Bigfoot was the target of many a Hill Country hunter for a while after that, but neither hide nor hair was seen of the creature again. If only Tom Sick and his team had been there!

But I may be doing Tom Slick an injustice to focus solely on his searches for abominable snowmen, Bigfoot and several other perhaps mythical creatures. This was a man who founded what is today the Southwest Foundation for Biomedical Research, the Institute of Inventive Research, the Southwest Research Institute and the Mind Science Foundation. Much of the work he founded continues today.

Slick helped develop Brangus cattle and at one time had one of the three largest herds of Angus cattle in the country. Following in the footsteps of his wildcatter father, he discovered the Benedum Field in west Texas, one of the largest oil strikes in the United States after World War II.

Most of us don't have any reasonable expectation of having Tom Slick's resources or of leaving such a legacy. What most of us have in common with Tom Slick is that we, too, want to know, once and for all, if there is or ever was such a creature as the yeti or Bigfoot. Like Tom Slick, we just want to know.

THE PLIGHT OF THE PLEUROCOELEUS

We don't usually think of dinosaurs when we think of Texas. We might think about the state's officially designated large mammal, the longhorn, or the state small mammal, the armadillo. We know that the state bird is the mockingbird, the state tree is the pecan and the horned lizard (or horny toad, as most of us call it) is the state reptile. Rock hounds might even know that the state stone is petrified palm wood. Seldom is heard a word, discouraging or otherwise, about the state dinosaur, the pleurocoeleus.

The pleurocoeleus is the official state dinosaur of Texas.

Whether Texas actually needs a state dinosaur is open to debate, but the pleurocoeleus (*Brachiosaur sauropod*) was so designated by the state legislature 1997. It's our dinosaur, by golly, and we're Texans, so we're going to be proud of it, even if it wasn't what you might call ferocious. You might think that Texas would have adopted a carnivore, but our dinosaur was a strict vegetarian. At least it was big—about fifty feet long and weighing in at about twenty tons. Paleontologists tell us that despite its size, our dinosaur was decidedly mild-mannered. Fight or flight? The pleurocoeleus probably didn't have to give the matter a lot of thought.

We can watch and listen to mockingbirds, pick pecans and we know a longhorn cow when we see one and an armadillo, which we can't always avoid when they try to cross the road. The pleurocoeleus hasn't been seen in these parts for, oh, about sixty-five million years, give or take a few million years either way. But we have proof that they lived here.

Near Glen Rose, at the appropriately named Dinosaur Valley State Park, on the banks of the Paluxy River and in the riverbed itself, are some remarkably well-preserved pleurocoeleus tracks. These are some of the best dinosaur tracks in the world, which is why paleontologists love the park and have ever since Roland T. Bird of the American Museum of Natural History visited the site in 1938. Bird realized that a set of double tracks showed an herbivorous sauropod—most likely our boy, the pleurocoeleus—being chased by a meat-eating carnosaur.

This was the first time sauropod tracks had been discovered anywhere in the world, which caused no small amount of excitement back in New York. The Glen Rose tracks were duly sent to New York and displayed at the American Museum of Natural History. The pleurocoelus obviously couldn't get away from the site fast enough on that particular day, but since then its tracks have been scattered hither and yon, to the Texas Memorial Museum in Austin and, unfortunately, into the private residences of many amateurs—or vandals, depending on how you look at these things.

The dinosaur tracks are a major wonder, but it's a small wonder that any tracks are left here at all. People complain that all the "good" tracks have been removed from the Paluxy River Valley. A woman in Glen Rose told me that a lot of area families have a quarried dinosaur track or two in their homes. "You usually see them on people's living room wall," she said.

It took a special set of circumstances to preserve the tracks for all these millions of years. Scientists believe that a violent storm blew across the shoreline a few days before the tracks were made and created a series of sand- and lime-laden mudflats. A herd of pleurocoelus came ambling across the sticky and still-wet mud in search of a primordial salad, followed in interested pursuit by the carnosaurs looking for some fresh sauropods; the pleurocoelus qualified.

True to their pacifistic nature, the pleurocoelus tried to run away, but we don't know if they won that particular footrace or not. No intact skeleton remains were ever found, just huge saucerlike depressions from their hind feet and smaller tracks, much like horseshoes, from their front legs.

The primal, existential struggle for food and survival was preserved in stone when the seashore turned to stone, leaving behind the rocks we see in the park today, including the ones with the dinosaur prints.

We in Texas have never collected dinosaur fossils like we have collected, say, arrowheads, but the state has had its fair share of fossilized dinosaur discoveries over the years due to a quirk of ancient geography dating back to when much of what is now Texas was covered by an ancient sea. As the sea level rose, the land was covered with ocean silt. Sediments on the bottom of the ocean preserved things that lived in the ocean. At lower sea levels, things that lived on land were preserved in sediments left in streams and rivers, like the Paluxy. Other tracks are preserved near Canyon Dam at the Museum of the Hill Country.

As a result, dinosaur discoveries in Texas have included both the marine and terrestrial, along with the ones that flew over land and sea. While having a state dinosaur might seem like a trivial thing—it is—and maybe even a waste of legislative time, it's not a bad idea to take official note of ancient Texas.

As Texans, we have always prided ourselves on our connection to the wild, whether it's wild Comanches or wild animals or wild land. And wildness is wildness, whether it's slinking across your pasture tonight or lived millions of years ago and you're literally walking in its footsteps.

ODE TO THE HORNY TOAD

The horned lizard—known to generations as horny toads—was named the state reptile of Texas in 1993, just in time for fire ants and a whole host of environmental factors to pretty much clear them from the landscape.

The main damage that fire ants have done to the horny toad is devouring its favorite food, the harvester ant. Insecticides aimed at controlling fire ants haven't done the horny toad any favors either, and they don't do well in urban and suburban environments.

That anything could eliminate the horny toad is almost unthinkable to a generation of Texans who grew up with them. For a lot of us, horny toads provided an early and direct link to nature. The fact that they looked like miniature monsters was a bonus. The short, pointed snout and rows of spikes, including two big ones in the middle of the head that look like horns, give the horned lizard a menacing and ferocious look that belies its gentle nature.

The State of Texas and biologists call it the Texas horned lizard, and most of the rest of us call it the horny toad, but on the campus of Texas Christian University in Fort Worth, the school's mascot is known as a "Horned Frog." The biologically correct have crusaded to have the mascot changed to its proper name, but the Horned Frogs of TCU will have none of it.

British diplomat Francis Sheridan once described the horny toad as "having the head of a frog, the back and belly of an alligator

The horned lizard, once a part of the everyday Texas landscape, has all but vanished in modern times. *Leroy Williamson.*

and the tail of a turtle." That's a pretty good description, especially for a British diplomat who was otherwise snide and condescending toward Texas.

That horny toads have become scarce is a surprising irony given that they are known in history and lore as magnificent survivors. The greatest survivor of his species is Ol' Rip, who supposedly survived thirty-one years, from 1897 to 1928, sealed into the cornerstone of the Eastland County Courthouse. When the old courthouse was torn down to make way for a new one, Ol' Rip blinked a couple of times, surveyed the situation and tried to scamper away.

"I know it happened because I saw it," one observer said. "I know it didn't happen because it just doesn't make sense."

Or does it?

Sam McInnis, a professor at Brownwood's Daniel Baker College, is inclined to believe the story. He wrote, "From what I know about the story I think that it is true, because the frog was entombed in sand and rock, and it is possible for moisture and oxygen to pass through the rock and reach the frog and sustain life for an indefinite period of time."

Ol' Rip's resurrection got as much coverage, in Texas newspapers anyway, as Charles Lindbergh's flight across the Atlantic Ocean. Ol' Rip went on tour with his own entourage and even met President Coolidge. Observers of the meeting were hard-pressed to say whether Coolidge or the Ol' Rip was the less talkative of the two.

After Ol' Rip died a second time, he was laid to rest in the lobby of the Eastland County Courthouse, where visitors can still see him today.

While it's easy to blame the horny toad's vanishing acts on the usual and aforementioned man-made and natural suspects, a lot of us who grew up loving the little critters might have helped loved them to death. In light of a more considerate age, when it's not even legal to possess a horny toad, carrying them around in our pockets and playing catch with them could not have done the species any good, not to mention the trauma to the individual horny toads. What can we say all these years later? We were kids and we didn't know.

Other pastimes were kinder and gentler. When you stroked their bellies, they went into a hypnotic trance. Hypnotizing a wild critter, even a little one, gave us a greater sense of power than being able to pick one up and put it in our pocket.

Most of the time, you could walk right up to a horny toad, pick it up, hypnotize it and put it in your pocket as a surprise for mom, and the horny toad didn't seem to mind. Occasionally, one would puff up until it looked like a spiny golf ball, but that was usually the extent of any resistance.

Old-timers told us that horny toads would "spit" blood out of their eyes when they got mad, but we enjoyed blood-free relations with the horny toads for years—until one day when one of them blinked at us and "spit" blood all over Ricky Park's t-shirt. We were suitably horrified, not only at what happened to Ricky but that the old-timers turned out to be right about something that had sounded so ridiculous.

As adults, we have been suitably horrified to recall how we collected and traded horny toads much the same way we traded baseball cards. Somebody said they saw one in a pet store one day, and the next time anybody mentioned horny toads, it was to say that they hadn't seen one in more than ten years.

Still, a lot of us can't help but hope that the whole species pulls an Ol' Rip on us and emerges from the darkness of near extinction to the point where we might even consider them a minor nuisance again, just because of their sheer numbers.

HOME WITH THE ARMADILLO

The armadillo was named the state's official small mammal by the Texas legislature in 1995 in recognition of the little critters semi-iconic status in Texas. The armadillo is more comic than iconic, but in a morbid sort of way; the unofficial name of the armadillo is *Roadkillibus Texanis*.

The nine-banded armadillo, the armadillo chosen for state designation and the one that might be digging up your garden or lawn right now, is not even native to Texas but has surely found a home here. Where else but Texas could a humble, nearsighted critter rise to become the official state small mammal?

A 1974 resolution to make the armadillo the state mammal read, in part: "The armadillo has grown and expanded with Texas and is now found all over the state from, from Terlingua to Bug Tussle and from Dumas to Atascosa, a hardy and busy animal, protector of the crops and fauna by the consumption of ants and other insects."

That resolution failed, as did subsequent efforts, but in 1981 the legislature decreed that the armadillo be recognized as the official state mascot. Finally, in 1995, the armadillo got its official state mammal designation. Some of us think that they had it right when they deemed it a mascot.

Armadillos moved from Mexico into the Rio Grande Valley about 150 years ago and then into the Hill Country by the early 1900s. For a while, armadillos were known as "Hoover hogs" to point out the fact that the country was so poor and hungry that people were reduced to eating armadillos and to blame the whole mess on President Herbert Hoover because the Depression had happened on his watch.

There has been a brisk trade for curios fashioned from the armadillo's shell, including baskets, wall hangings and ashtrays. Writer, musician and erstwhile candidate for governor Kinky Friedman says that he hopes there is an alternate universe where armadillos make ashtrays out of people.

The armadillo has few natural predators, unless you count motorized vehicles. When frightened, armadillos jump right straight up in the air like a cartoon critter. In the field, it's comical. On the road, it's deadly; they tend to jump right into the undercarriage of the car or truck that they don't see or hear until it's right on top of them.

Armadillos are good and adaptable swimmers, but even there they show some cartoonish characteristics, like walking across the bottom of a

Though not native to the state, the legislature has deemed the humble armadillo the official state small mammal. *Leroy Williamson.*

creek or narrow river. They can also "inflate" and make themselves more buoyant if they prefer to move across the top of the water.

The part of that 1974 resolution about the armadillo being a protector of crops and fauna may seem way off base to anyone who has had an armadillo tear up the yard or garden. Armadillos use their noses to dig up grubs and other delicacies. They see well enough for that activity but not well enough to see somebody walk over and pick them up by the tail. (By the way, doing that is strongly discouraged; recent medical research indicates that handling armadillos might increase a person's exposure to leprosy. Armadillos have very little immunity to this disease.)

The armadillo as a Texas symbol took off in the 1970s, fueled by the popularity of the Armadillo World Headquarters music hall in Austin and the art of Jim Franklin, who was dubbed the "Michelangelo of armadillo art." One of Franklin's most famous paintings was located at Armadillo World Headquarters. The painting depicted an armadillo emerging from blues guitarist Freddy King's heart as he played his guitar. A popular song of the day, one adopted as the theme song to the *Austin City Limits* TV show on PBS, expressed a desire to leave England and go "home with the Armadillo," a reference to Armadillo World Headquarters.

A fellow by the name of Sam Lewis did a lot to link the armadillo to Texas. Lewis, who died in 2003 at age eighty, staged armadillo races around the world and founded the Armadillo Appreciation Society. He took an armadillo with him everywhere he went.

None of this holds much sway with people who have an armadillo wreaking havoc around the house or in the fields. It's not like they're feral hogs, but armadillos can do a considerable amount of damage in a short amount of time.

The bad news is that there's not a lot most people can do about a delinquent armadillo, other than calling up a professional animal removal service. Picking them up by the tail and taking them somewhere else used to be a good idea, but now there's that leprosy thing.

A good fence helps, and ultrasonic pest deterrents that might or might not work are on the market. You can trap it and move it to another location. Mothballs can keep armadillos out of a small garden or patch of turf because their sensitive noses can't stand the stuff. Other than that, you just have to wait for that armadillo to find its way to the nearest road or highway.

A BLUEBONNET BY ANY OTHER NAME

Depending on how taxonomically correct you want to be, you could say that Texas has at least five state flowers—and all of them are bluebonnets. That is the result of a drawn-out legislative process that, for seventy years, included some bluebonnets in its designation, but not all of them.

The Colonial Dames of Texas pushed the state legislature to adopt the bluebonnet as the official state flower in 1901 but met with immediate opposition. What had seemed like an innocuous legislative formality brought forth dissent from, among others, John Nance Garner of Uvalde. Garner, who would later serve as vice president under Franklin Roosevelt, was passionate and articulate in boosting his choice for the state flower, the prickly pear bloom. He was thereafter known as "Cactus Jack," and the name stuck. Another group wanted to adopt the open cotton boll as the "white flower of commerce."

For a time, it looked like the bluebonnet's future as a floral symbol of Texas might be doomed, but a painting of a field of bluebonnets by Miss Modie Walker of Austin, presented by the Dames in support

The bluebonnet, the state flower of Texas, provides a blanket of blue and a lot of photo opportunities each spring for people in the Hill Country. *Leroy Williamson.*

of their flower, swayed the opposition, and the bluebonnets won the day. Or so it seemed. As hard as it may be to imagine, people actually accused the state legislature of making a mistake; the darn fools picked the wrong bluebonnet.

The flower named in the 1901 resolution was the species of bluebonnet classified as *Lupinus subcarnosus*, commonly referred to in those days as buffalo clover, because it was thought that buffalo ate the plant. Like their bovine successors, buffalo actually don't care much for bluebonnets, but sheep and goats will eat them 'til the cows come home.

Botanists, florists and people who just plain knew their wildflowers insisted that the resolution should have specified the *Lupinus texensis*, or Texas bluebonnet, and it's hard to find fault with their belief that a species named for the state is the logical and correct choice for the state flower. Since the adoption of the state flower is something of a beauty contest, opponents to the wording of the original legislation insisted that *Lupinus subcarnosus* is not nearly as pretty as the Texas bluebonnet, the one that carpets fields throughout most of Texas every spring. Seventy years after the state legislature's original choice, the 1971 legislature amended the adoption to include the Texas bluebonnet and "any other varieties of Bluebonnet not heretofore recorded."

The legislators might have thought that they had settled the matter, but only because they didn't know or didn't care that we have at least three other species of bluebonnets in the state. People from east or central Texas would recognize a species known commonly as the Big Bend or Chisos bluebonnet as the state flower, but they might think it was on some kind of botanical steroids; it grows three to four feet high and has flowers a deep blue with a lemon blotch. It stays put in the Trans-Pecos region and doesn't care to grow wild or cultivated anywhere else.

Another variety, with the common name of Bajada bluebonnet, doesn't look much like a bluebonnet at all. The Lady Bird Johnson Wildflower Center describes it as "a somewhat sprawling lupine." In the Panhandle, *Lupinus lattensis* is known as the Plains bluebonnet or Nebraska bluebonnet. It's not as showy as the Texas bluebonnet and grows to be about two feet tall. But it's still a bluebonnet.

People used to call the bluebonnet a "wolf flower" instead of a wildflower because it was believed that bluebonnets robbed the soil the same way a wolf robs a flock of sheep. Once the question was put to a test, it was discovered that bluebonnets actually benefit the soil by adding nitrogen. Legislators can be glad that the bluebonnet wasn't found to be obnoxious or invasive. No one likes that in a state flower. Something would have to be done.

As it is, the Texas bluebonnet is vigorously supported by the highway department, which plants them along Texas roadsides, and garden club members, which plant them everywhere they can. Businesses, historical societies and organizations use "bluebonnet" in their name to identify the enterprise as having something to do with Texas. "It's not only the state flower but also kind of a floral trademark almost as well known to outsiders as cowboy boots and the Stetson hat," longtime Texas columnist and author Jack Maguire once wrote. "The bluebonnet is to Texas what the shamrock is to Ireland, the cherry blossom to Japan, the lily to France, the rose to England and tulip to Holland."

Besides, it's hard to imagine generations of Texas families sitting their babies in a field of prickly pear or the middle of a cotton field to pose for an obligatory springtime picture. We have bluebonnets for that. The state flower of Texas, by any other name, would still be a bluebonnet, regardless of what kind of bluebonnet it might happen to be.

Part IV

TEXAS ORIGINALS

FROM SAD IRONS TO BIG DAMS

In 1917, the all-male voting population of Burnet elected Ophelia (Birdie) Crosby Harwood the first female mayor in the United States. Most Hill Country women didn't have those opportunities.

Women are not well represented in many histories of the Hill Country, probably because they were too busy for recorded history. The things most of the women did most of the time were unglamorous and unheralded: hauling water, tending fires, washing clothes and canning fruits and vegetables. In the early days, they often had to fight Indians, too.

In his biography of President Lyndon Johnson, author Robert Caro—with the aid of his wife—put together an astonishing account of day-to-day life for Hill Country women in the early and mid-twentieth century, just a couple of generations ago. Caro believed that to understand LBJ and why he was a successful politician, one had to first understand where he came from, what day-to-day life was like in the Hill Country where he grew up and how the life that was lived and the land it was lived on helped shape Johnson's character and political future.

His grandfather was Sam Ealy Johnson, who bought some land along the Pedernales River in 1882 and settled there with his wife, Eliza. The future president would be born in a small white ranch house on that property on August 27, 1908. Johnson, who has been called "the last of

The notation on the back of this photo read: "Mountain woman near Austin, Texas." *Library of Congress, from the Alan Lomax Collection.*

the frontier presidents," is said to have forever regretted that he was not born in a log cabin. He apparently regretted that none of his ancestors fought at either the Alamo or San Jacinto because he was known to lie vividly and recklessly on that subject. Lyndon's father, Sam Ealy Johnson Jr., and his new bride, Rebekah Baines, settled on the property in 1907.

Sam Ealy Johnson Sr. became partners with his brother, Tom, in a cattle operation after the Civil War. The war had greatly increased the number of unattended cattle running loose all over the state at a time when a steer worth six to ten dollars in Texas was bringing thirty to forty dollars in Kansas City. The Johnson brothers commenced running cattle to Kansas and cashing in on the bonanza. Sam was able to buy the land where he and Eliza and their children lived and later added a 640-acre adjoining tract. Not long after that, the great numbers of cattle making it to the northern markets depressed the price of beef to the point that he eventually sold the land to a nephew, James Polk Johnson, and tried to start over in Caldwell and then Hays County before returning to the Pedernales in 1889. He spent his life as a working cowboy.

Johnson grew up listening to stories from his grandfather about the rewards and perils of trailing an unruly herd of longhorns north, of stampedes and of dangerous river crossings. He heard how his grandmother, Eliza, paralyzed and bedridden when LBJ knew her, was alone in the house with an infant when the Indians came calling. She stuffed a handkerchief in the baby's mouth to keep its cries from being heard and hid under a trapdoor while Indians ransacked the house above. His grandfather died not long after Lyndon and his family moved to Johnson City, where he lived until he left to attend college in San Marcos. Johnson ran for Congress in 1937 to fill the tenth Congressional seat left vacant by the death of James Buchanan. Running on the promise to use electricity from dams being built in the Hill Country to bring electricity to that region, he defeated nine other candidates.

Life improved dramatically for people in the Hill Country, but especially the women, when electricity came to the Hill Country; as Caro pointed out, "Without electricity, even boiling water was work." In a land of relatively few windmills, water was hauled by hand from a well or creek and carried to the house. It took about forty gallons of water a day to run a farm in that place and time, which meant a lot of trips from the well to the house. Lyndon's reluctance to help his mother with pumping and hauling water was a source of friction between the future president and his father, Sam Ealy Johnson Jr.

To then boil the water, wood had to be cut and hauled to the house, where it was burned in wood-burning stoves that were notoriously slow to "start up" and were also known for covering the inside of the house in soot and ash, which had to be cleaned. (Johnson was also reluctant to help his mother with the wood hauling.) Once the stoves finally heated up, they made the house feel like a furnace, especially in the middle of an already brutal summer. The stoves had to be lit not only to boil water but also for cooking and canning. At least twice a day during canning, the ash container had to be wrestled outside, emptied and brought back. "And when the housewife wasn't bending down to the flames, she was standing over them," Caro wrote.

Whether it was canning season—usually the summer—or any other time of year, washing had to be done. The clothes were washed outside, where a huge vat of boiling water was suspended over a bigger fire. Clothes were scrubbed in one tub with handmade lye soap and swished around by means of broomstick or paddle. From there, the clothes went into a rinse tub and a bluing pan, followed by the starching, which completed the first of what was usually four or so loads per week. The tubs had to be changed, too, which took about eight gallons of water. By the end of the day, it was time to get more water and haul it back.

Many of the Hill Country women Caro talked to told him that of all the chores that befell them, ironing was the most onerous. "Washing was hard work, but ironing was the worst," one woman said. "Nothing could ever be as hard as ironing."

Wielding an iron in those days meant tossing around six- or seven-pound wedges of iron, often without handles, that had to be heated over a fire, where soot sometimes accumulated and, despite every effort, sent another garment back to the original washing tub. Also despite every effort, women burned their hands from time to time, which didn't excuse them from hauling six- and seven-pound loads of clothes around all day. "The women of the Hill Country never called the instruments they used every Tuesday 'irons,' they called them 'sad irons,'" Caro wrote.

Life was like that for people in the country because in the 1930s only 2.3 percent of the farms in Texas had electricity. Thirty years later, only two percent were without it. In between came the Rural Electrification Act of 1938, part of President Franklin Roosevelt's New Deal program, and Lyndon Johnson making sure that the Hill Country got its fair share of electricity.

The first of a series of dammed lakes that make up the Highland Lakes chain, Buchanan Dam was completed in 1938 and named for James Buchanan, the man who preceded Johnson in Congress. One of the lakes, Granite Shoals, was renamed Lake LBJ in 1965 while Johnson was president. The other lakes are Inks Lake, Lake Marble Falls, Lake Travis, Lake Austin and Lady Bird Lake, formerly known as Lake Austin. The lakes have helped make the Hill Country one of the top tourist and retirement destinations in the state and have probably done more to transform the Hill Country than any other thing. Without electricity, it never would have happened.

Sharpshooters Ad and Plinky Toepperwein

Adolph ("Ad") Toepperwein wasn't exactly born with a gun in his hand, which is probably a good thing for everybody involved, but he was the son of a gunsmith and knew how to handle a firearm from about the time he was big enough to hold one. In an earlier time, his talents would have been in high demand, but making a living with the gun wasn't as easy as it had been in frontier times.

Though Toepperwein's father specialized in making rifles for use by buffalo hunters, the buffalo had been hunted to the brink of extinction by the time young Toepperwein came of age. Hired guns like Johnny Ringo and his ilk had long since been declared liabilities by the same society that once hired them. Professional opportunities in the shooting business were limited.

Toepperwein, born in Boerne and raised in nearby Leon Springs, grew up hunting and target shooting and then tried working in a crockery shop and as a cartoonist for a San Antonio newspaper. He figured that he might be able to make a living by doing the thing he loved to do after he saw famed marksman "Doc" W.F. Carter at one of Buffalo Bill Cody's Wild West Shows. The young Toepperwein felt he could not only duplicate Carter's feats but exceed them, too. When a shootist known as Captain Bartlett broke Carter's records, Toepperwein predicted that he would someday beat that record as well.

Toepperwein found work at a theatre in San Antonio where the manager, George Walker, was so impressed with the young man's shooting ability that he paid Toepperwein's way to New York City in hopes that the trigger-happy young Texan might find work in vaudeville.

He did, but barely. A lot of young men of that time from all over the country had grown up shooting, were quite good at it and were also trying to make a living with their trigger fingers. Toepperwein created his own big break by closing down the shooting galleries at Coney Island simply by shooting hundreds of times without missing. The galleries he didn't clear of prize merchandise closed their doors before Toepperwein could get there. People paid attention, which caught the attention of a theatrical agent who signed Toepperwein to the Orin Brothers Circus. Billed as "Dead Eye Dick" in vaudeville circles, Toepperwein put on shooting exhibitions all over the United States and Mexico for the next eight years.

Ad and Plinky Toepperwein were a couple of straight shooters. *www. showmanshooter.com.*

In 1901, Toepperwein left the vaudeville and circus life and went to work for the Winchester Repeating Arms Company, staging exhibitions featuring Winchester rifles. He did that for fifty years and in the process established himself as the world's greatest marksman. He even combined his talent for drawing with his talent for firearms by shooting portraits in a matter of seconds into a square of tin. It became one of his trademarks. Ad also helped his wife, Elizabeth, become one of the world's top female sharpshooters.

Elizabeth Servaty worked as a cartridge assembler at Winchester's New Haven, Connecticut plant when she met Ad Toepperwein in 1903 and married him just a few weeks later. Though Elizabeth had never so much as fired a gun before she met Ad, she became a part of his act by becoming one of the world's best female sharpshooters. Publicity agents Americanized their last name and billed them as "the Famous

Topperwines." She was so good that there was debate about which of the Toepperweins was the better shot.

Ad set his first world's sharpshooting record at the St. Louis Fair in 1904. Two years later, in the course of a three-day exhibit, he successfully shot 19,999 out of 20,000 hand-thrown wooden blocks; no explanation has ever been made for the one he missed. What is widely considered to be the best shooting exhibition ever staged took place December 13–22, 1907, in San Antonio. During that ten-day stretch, shooting three Winchester .22 automatics for seven hours a day, Toepperwein missed just 9 of 72,500 wood blocks thrown in the air. A foreign enemy or a band of outlaws could have taken over the city by the end of it, because Toepperwein used up every piece of available ammunition in the course of the exhibition. It was during this exhibition that he made good on his youthful boasts, besting the records of Carver and Captain Bartlett, just as he had bragged that he would do. Of course, it's not bragging if you actually do it.

The Famous Topperwines toured together for more than forty years. She was called "Plinky" because the first time she successfully shot a tin can, she responded to the noise it made by saying, "I plinked it!" She went on to plink a lot of targets, at one point setting the world endurance trapshooting record by hitting 1,952 of 2,000 in five hours and twenty minutes. She was inducted into the trapshooting hall of fame in Vandalia, Ohio, in 1969.

Ad Toepperwein conducted shooting camps in Leon Springs after he retired from the Winchester Company in 1951 and was elected to the Texas Sports Hall of Fame. He died in San Antonio in 1962 and is buried next to Plinky in Mission Burial Park.

According to some people, Ad Toepperwein was not the best marksman that Leon Springs ever produced. Many, including Ad himself, said that his cousin, Rudolph Aue, was the best shot he had ever seen.

Rudolph was the son of Max Aue, sort of a legendary character in his own right. Max came to America from Germany in 1852, a veteran of the 1848 Schhleswig-Holstein War in northern Germany. He was further seasoned by a stint as a Texas Ranger, for which the state awarded him a 640-acre land grant in Leon Springs. He died in 1903 with more than 20,000 acres. He was considered the best hunter in the Hill Country and once was part of a posse that caught and killed the men who robbed his store.

Rudolph refused to shoot professionally because he said it was just a waste of good ammunition. Ad's famous San Antonio demonstration, which exhausted an entire city's ammunition, could probably be used to make his point. Ad Toepperwein once wrote this line about his cousin: "I've traveled around the world but no one could shoot like Rudy could."

OLD YELLER COUNTRY

If Fred Gipson could return to Mason now, thirty-five years after his death, he would still recognize the town and, more importantly to him, the surrounding countryside. Unlike much of the Texas Hill Country, which is being transformed or even lost on an almost daily basis, Mason still retains a certain timeless quality.

For people of a certain age, it's hard not to see Mason County as *Old Yeller* country. Gipson gave the world the novel by that name fifty-two years ago. The novel and the movie classic of the same name changed the rules in children's literature and entertainment; happy endings were no longer required.

A friend once told me that when he was young and single he would give his girlfriends a copy of *Old Yeller* to read. The ones who didn't cry when they finished the book were written off as potential lifetime mates.

Gipson wrote half a dozen other books, most of them set as firmly in the Mason County soil as the large blocks of granite that dot the landscape. Before Larry McMurtry came along, Gipson was Texas's best-selling author of all time. Unlike a lot of other writers, Gipson never stayed gone from his home county for long. His best friend, Joe Austell Small, related in the introduction to Mike Cox's biography of Gipson a time when he and Gipson spent an idyllic few days fishing for tarpon in Mexico. As guests of a wealthy businessman, Gipson and Small, for a few days, lived a life that Gipson described as being as close to paradise as a person was likely to get. The next day, he told an incredulous Small that it was time to go back home.

"This was a part of Fred that I finally became accustomed to," Small wrote. "Never a homing pigeon had a stronger and more emotional desire to return than Fred Gipson."

Poster for the
movie version of
Fred Gipson's *Old
Yeller*.

While *Old Yeller* will always be Gipson's literary calling card, his best work of fiction is probably his first novel, *Hound Dog Man*. That book, with its subtle but vivid descriptions of the natural world and man's relation to it, is an overlooked classic, eclipsed by the immense popularity of *Old Yeller*. *Hound Dog Man* gives the reader a deeper insight into what made Gipson tick, as a man and as a writer, than any of his other works. It is the equivalent of a Texas *Huckleberry Finn*.

Fred Gipson was fly-fishing Texas rivers when such a thing was almost unheard of. As a young newspaper writer, he once wrote about the healing properties of fishing. "Fishing makes a man feel like a boy again," Gipson wrote. "If old Ponce De Leon had just forgotten all about his 'fountain of youth' and come to Texas with a cane pole and a can of worms, he wouldn't have died all disappointed and heartbroken like he did."

In an acceptance speech he wrote for the 1959 Young Reader's Choice Award, which the Pacific Northwest Library Association awarded him for *Old Yeller*, Gipson described his motivation to write the book—to simply tell a good story that he hoped readers of all ages would enjoy—before taking on a more personal tone in describing the joy he derives from nature. Perhaps more than anything else he wrote, that acceptance speech gives voice to what made Fred Gipson tick, as a writer and as a man:

> *I like to watch the wind-waves running across the grass. I like to watch the approach of a turbulent thunderstorm. I like to hear quail calling to each other when I wake up in the mornings; I like to see the high-flying geese riding the lift of the first cold front to come rolling out of the north at the beginning of winter.*
>
> *I like to listen to the trail-cry of a bell-voiced hound driving hard after a fox—to watch hummingbirds feeding among the yard flowers while I shell a mess of black-eyed peas for supper. I like the smell of new-mown hay—the rank scent of a sweaty horse—the blaring of old range cows, calling to their calves—the swift flight of wild doves seeking their roosts in the afterglow of sunset.*
>
> *I like to see the flirt of a buck deer's tail as he charges into a brush thicket, to listen to the yelp of a wild gobbler down in a deep canyon, to hear the tail-popping splash of a feeding bass as he breaks the surface of a quiet pool.*
>
> *To me, these things have meaning. They give me a lift of the spirit in a way that no man-made thing has ever done. They are basic, elemental, and eternal. I think they will be here long after I'm gone—and after you are gone.*
>
> *In my books, I write of those things that have meaning to me, hoping to communicate to my readers some understanding and appreciation for the rightness and fitness of a world that man seems furiously bent upon destroying.*

ROY BEDICHEK: TEXAS ORIGINAL

Of the three men who made up Texas's early literary triumvirate—J. Frank Dobie, Walter Prescott Webb and Roy Bedichek—Bedichek was the last one to publish a book (when he was sixty-nine years old) and the least known of the three during his day. Time and new generations of readers have turned that around to the point where Bedichek's one significant book—*Adventures with a Texas Naturalist*—has outlived most of the books written by Dobie and Webb.

The spirit of independence, inquiry and originality that make the book remarkable are among the same qualities that made Bedichek the person so remarkable as well. He has been called the state's "most civilized soul," and in a state full of originals, he still stands out.

"Bedichek was, simply, one of the most interesting and unique people in Texas," Steven L. Davis writes in his new book, *J. Frank Dobie: A Liberated Mind*. Dobie and Webb held the same view of Bedi, as they called him, and not only urged him to write his book about the natural world but also spearheaded a fundraising effort so he could take a year off from work to do so.

That effort and what Bedichek did with the opportunity have paid off for subsequent generations of Texans by leaving us with Bedichek's wholly original thoughts on nature, art and life and how they—and everything else—are intertwined. In *Adventures with a Texas Naturalist*, he walks that thin line between art and science, between hard fact and pure passion. He reveres both and has little patience for those who indulge one at the expense of the other. "I sometimes think we have become dominated by a cult of unemotionalism," he wrote. "We speak of 'cold' scientific fact as if temperature had something to do with verity."

Bedichek was never in danger of joining that cult of unemotionalism. That is nowhere more evident in a passage that begins with a simple statement about the Inca dove. "The Inca has a curious call, monotonously repeated, especially in morning hours, all through the spring months. Nothing quite like it comes from the throat of any other bird or beast," he wrote. Then he goes on to relate a remarkable story about a man in an Austin nursing home and how an Inca dove brought the two men together.

Roy Bedichek, a lifelong naturalist, didn't publish his first book until he was sixty-nine years old, but it has become an enduring classic. *www.bedichek.org*

The keeper of the nursing home called Bedichek one night and asked if he was the man who knew the name of birds, and Bedichek allowed as how he might be. The woman asked Bedichek for help with a patient who was unable to sleep for trying to figure out the song of a particular bird he kept hearing outside of his window. Bedichek went to see the man the next day and found a "palsied, bed-ridden gentleman, whose speech was rendered almost unintelligible by his ailment." Bedichek eventually hears the birdsong and identifies it as the Inca dove. The man relaxes upon hearing this, mutters a sigh of thanks and falls asleep.

The man, it turned out, was a botanist whose intense love for and curiosity about the natural world matched Bedichek's. After the man recovered from his ailment, he and Bedichek began taking trips into the Hill Country, just to have a look around and talk about things. "He was interested not only in the mechanism, but also in the mysterious force that uses mechanism for its occult purposes," Bedichek wrote of the man who, on one of these trips, expressed sadness upon seeing a patch of Mexican evening primroses cut down. "They're such friendly flowers— they creep right up to your door," the man lamented.

So does the Inca dove, Bedichek noted. "Since then I never see a patch of flowers and never hear an Inca dove without a memory of this fine old character, trembling with palsy on the brink of the grave but still, like a youth, in love with sun and flowers and birds and generally with the out-of-doors," Bedichek concluded. He could just as easily have been describing himself with the latter part of that passage.

Until his book was published, most people in the state knew Bedichek as director of the University Interscholastic League, which was set up to regulate athletic and academic competitions in Texas schools. He served in that capacity for twenty-six years, from 1922 to 1948.

Bedichek, who rarely ate meat unless it was cooked over an open fire and who eschewed pesticides in his own garden, distrusted doctors and was rarely ill until he died in 1959 at the age of eighty-one while waiting for his wife Lillian's cornbread to come out of the oven. His old friends admired the manner of his going and considered it all together in character with this Texas original. In a wistful letter to his departed friend, Webb wrote, "Few people are able to call their own shots as you did, right up to the end."

EVERYBODY'S SOMEBODY IN LUCKENBACH

Contrary to what you might think from reading stories about Luckenbach, Texas, it's not a rule that anyone writing about Luckenbach has to mention "Willie, Waylon and the boys" in the first line. Luckenbach existed outside the realm of pop culture for more than one hundred years before the song "Luckenbach, Texas," as recorded by Willie Nelson and Waylon Jennings, put the town on the cultural map in 1977.

Even with that *Hit Parade* kind of fame, Luckenbach is still the kind of town you can miss if you happen to blink when you drive past. In case you don't know, Luckenbach is a small town. How small is it? "It's so small, even the mice are stoop shouldered," my friend Ernie Earnest said when we first visited the place in 1973, and several times afterward.

The "official" population is three, which has held more or less steady since the town's patron saint, Hondo Crouch, along with Guich Koock and Kathy Morgan, bought the town and its one parking meter in response to

Luckenbach, where everybody is somebody.

a classified ad in a San Antonio newspaper in 1970. Population estimates these days run from three to twenty-five, depending on who you ask and his definition of a resident.

Crouch and Luckenbach were a natural fit. Crouch was an all-American swimmer at the University of Texas in the late 1930s. For twelve years, he wrote a column for the *Comfort News* under the name "Peter Cedarstacker" in which he was an equal-opportunity satirist, taking on everything from government and politics to deer hunters and the everyday travails of country life. Crouch was the unofficial mayor of Luckenbach. He used to say, "People can't believe we have such a big moon for such a small town." The local paper, published every so often, is called the *Luckenbach Moon* in honor of that observation.

Hondo's mantra was "Everybody is somebody in Luckenbach." That sentiment is printed on bumper stickers and T-shirts and is the town's unofficial motto. Luckenbach is about the most unofficial place you are likely to find. Simply being unincorporated has never been enough for Luckenbach. The town was founded as a trading post in 1849 and was known to serve Comanches, as well as pioneer farmers and ranchers. Even then, everybody was somebody in Luckenbach. Even Comanches.

If you are somebody who likes Texas music, you will find like-minded sensibilities in Luckenbach about any day of the week. Truth is, if you don't like Texas music, this might not be destination for you. You would still be somebody, but you might be somebody wondering how many steps there are in a Texas two-step.

Today, downtown Luckenbach consists of a bar, a dance hall and a gift shop disguised as a post office. Out front of the gift shop is a Texas historical marker and a sculpture of Hondo Crouch his own self. The dance hall keeps the town going. Built in 1886, it was renovated in 1935 with a solid maple floor. Various publications have dubbed it the best dance hall in Texas, and it was featured prominently in the Smithsonian exhibit Dance Halls and Last Calls.

After Crouch and his cronies bought the town, painters and other assorted artists started hanging out there, and the idea of an arts and crafts festival was suggested. That was too tame for Crouch and his friends, so they decided to stage a world's fair in Luckenbach. Of course, it was an unofficial world's fair. The highlight of the festivities came when various citizens took turns firing cannons at an outhouse until it had been completely obliterated. There have been other extravaganzas, like a chili cook-off for women only, a no-talent contest and some festival dedicated, as I understand it, to mud daubers. Jerry Jeff Walker recorded his hit album *Viva Terlingua* there in the early '70s, and Willie and Waylon and the boys got involved a few years later.

It had been years since I'd been to Luckenbach, so I stopped in not long ago when I was in the area. Half a dozen or so people were gathered in the bar, picking and singing and knocking back a couple of cold ones to pass the afternoon. The sign over the bar read: "If you're drinking to forget, please pay in advance." Another one suggested that if you need credit you need a job more than you need a beer.

Sure, Luckenbach is not exactly what it used to be, but few places are; time insists on doing its job. Thieves have taken off with some of the old signs and an antique fire truck. Floods have taken the old cotton gin and the blacksmith shop. Two of the town's most vivid, respected and respectable characters, Crouch and (unofficial) Sheriff Marge Mueller, have passed on.

There have been other changes. A bed-and-breakfast on Ranch Road 1376 does a brisk business on weekends, and somebody has cobbled together a small shopping complex on the same road called "Uptown Luckenbach." Asked if they thought Hondo Crouch would have approved of such a place, no one in Luckenbach cared to comment that day.

Leaving, it occurred to me that for such a small place, Luckenbach has created a lot of good memories for a lot of people. You can't ask much more of a place than that. As Hondo used to say, "You can't forget memories."

THE BAMBERGER PLACE

When David Bamberger bought the first parcel of his Hill Country Ranch in 1969, the county's Soil Conservation Service agent delivered a blunt assessment.

"Bamberger, I don't know why you bought it," the agent said. "It will take forty-three acres of this land to support one cow. There's not a drop of water. You just bought the worst property in Blanco County." That first three thousand acres was covered in Ashe juniper—commonly called cedar—and the only water to be found on the ranch was "gyp water" the color of a Bloody Mary.

Today, the ranch is used as a model of what can be accomplished with land stewardship. Most of the cedar was removed and replaced with grass. Dozens of springs and seeps that hadn't been seen for decades emerged from a long dormancy and today supply enough water to support four families, thousands of visitors, two hundred cows and five hundred goats; there is enough left over for a small lake and a couple of dozen stock tanks.

In the years since that initial investment, Bamberger's land stewardship has been recognized with awards from the Texas Service, the Audubon Society, the Natural Resources Conservation Service and the Texas Commission on Environmental Quality. The ranch, which recently received the Lone Star Land Stewards Regional Award, has gone from the worst property in Blanco County to one of the best in

David Bamberger turned his property from the "worst piece of land in Blanco County" to a highly regarded example of environmental stewardship. *Author photo.*

the country and now includes more than 5,500 acres. Since 2002, it has operated as the Bamberger Ranch Preserve in order to protect it from further development.

The secret, Bamberger said during a recent visit to his ranch, which he named Selah, is grass. "Grass is the most important tool for ranch economics," Bamberger, eighty, said while walking through the one expanse of cedar that he keeps around to show visitors what the whole ranch looked like when he bought it. "Grass is the greatest conservation tool there is. Grass is the answer if you have a piece of unproductive land."

Bamberger, who made his fortune as a cofounder of the Church's Fried Chicken chain, said he spent a fortune on grass seed after he removed enough of the cedar to plant grass. "I would never do that again," he said of buying grass seed. He switched from buying seed to harvesting it in autumn from roadsides and fields, which he recommends to anyone wanting to revitalize a piece of unproductive property.

Two and a half years after he started clearing the cedar and planting grass, the first spring showed up on his property as a damp green spot. He and Leroy Petri, who has been crucial to the work Bamberger has accomplished at Selah, dug out the spring, encased it in cement and connected PVC pipe from the spring to the house. He would later add a cistern and more storage space until he could store twenty-two thousand gallons of water from that one spring. Even during the worst of recent droughts, the Bamberger Ranch has never been without water. "That's the lesson of Selah," he said. "That's what the land has taught me, that if you take care of the land, the land will provide for you."

"Selah" is a Biblical term taken from the Psalms that asks readers to pause and reflect on the message. At Selah, visitors are invited to pause and reflect on the natural world.

Bamberger said that the agricultural part of his operation is profitable and that he could make a living from it if he chose, but he has opened up the ranch to visitors (by appointment) and devoted much of his resources to education because he believes that what he has learned at Selah is important and that future generations can learn the importance of preserving the natural world.

Part of the educational component can be seen near the banks of Madrone Lake, where he has rigged up a rainfall simulator—he calls it a "rain machine"—to demonstrate how rainfall affects land planted in grasses opposed to land that is mostly cedar, with very little grass. The simulator uses PVC pipe to distribute the equivalent of a one-inch rainfall to two trays, one with bare soil and cedar saplings and the other with a healthy clump of little bluestem grass. A funnel for runoff at the base of each tray collects runoff in one jar and groundwater in another. A few minutes after the rain machine is activated, the runoff jar beneath the tray with the cedar saplings fills with dirty brown water while the jar underneath the tray with grass has just a few drops. The groundwater jar under the grass tray fills with clear water.

"If visitors to the ranch don't take anything else away from their visit, I want them to understand the importance that this little rain machine demonstrates," he said. "Going from a cedar brake to a prairie is how this land was transformed into what it is today. This is a fundamental demonstration of what happens to land when it rains, and why some soil washes away and other pieces of land experience very little runoff, even during a heavy rain."

Bamberger admits that not everybody who buys a piece of land is going to want thousands of visitors each year. "You have to have the 'people gene,'" he said. "Some people don't want anybody on their land for any reason at all. My brother in Oklahoma is like that. He says to me, 'I work to keep people off my land. I don't know why you invited all these people out to your place.' It's just different ways of looking at things. Before anybody buys land, they should know what they want from it and how to go about getting it."

Some of the people who visit the Bamberger Ranch each year are hunters, which have become a key part of many ranching operations in central Texas and the Hill Country. Here, too, Bamberger says that the improvement of the land led to a dramatic improvement:

> I first leased this out to hunters forty years ago. I had some customers the first year, but the phone didn't ring the second year. Nobody was coming back. I called up one fellow who had hunted here and asked him if he planned on coming back, and he said no, that the only deer he killed the year before was fifty-five pounds.
>
> Last year I took in $103,000 from hunting, and the smallest deer we had was 116 pounds. That didn't happen by accident. It happened

because we brought back the grasses and other vegetation that deer depend on.

Though he is eighty years old, it's hard to keep up with Bamberger once he starts showing a visitor his ranch. There are stops at Hes' Country Store, named in honor of his mother, and treks up one nature trail or another to show off his efforts to save the Texas Snowbell, an endangered Texas plant, along with the madrone and big-tooted maple trees he has planted.

Along the way are stops at a chiroptorium—a bat cave that he had constructed on his land, which is now home to thousands of bats—and a pasture with Scimitar-Horned Oryx, which he raises as part of a program to return the species to its native habitat. He stops at another place to show how landowners who want an ag exemption but aren't necessarily into cows can get the exemption through other methods, like creating wildlife habitat and conducting bird counts. Each stop, it seems, is a separate, full-blown story and part of the four decades he has put into this land.

"Don't start anything you don't intend to stay with," he says.

Even some of the projects that have not succeeded—like his line of Grassmaster cattle and a plan to distribute "beef candy bars" to the needy—entailed years if not decades of labor. He said he doesn't regret any of it, even the projects that didn't work out, because he learned something from everything that he tried.

"It's hard to make a good living off land like this strictly from agriculture, but there are other opportunities," he said. "People will pay money to see wildlife, not just exotic wildlife, but the everyday animals that you can support on a place like this without even trying…If you're people-oriented, you can learn the grasses, trees, and birds and become a naturalist, and interpret nature to outsiders. You give people something they don't get in their everyday lives, and you contribute something to society."

THANKSGIVING AS A TEXAS THANG

Even if Texans wrote the history of Thanksgiving, arguments would persist over where in Texas the alleged feast took place and when. In one corner would be the group proclaiming May 23, 1541, as the date of the first Thanksgiving and Palo Duro Canyon as the site. Spanish explorer Coronado would be the star of legend and lore, and we'd probably be eating leftover buffalo instead of turkey. In the other corner would be the people proclaiming an April 30, 1598 feast along the Rio Grande the first Thanksgiving.

Both stories center on travesties, travails and encounters with two of the most forbidding landscapes Texas has to offer—the Llano Estacado and the Chihuahuan Desert. Surviving a sixteenth-century trek across either landscape would be cause for thanks aplenty.

The Palo Duro camp tells us that on May 23, 1541, a friar traveling with the Coronado expedition proposed a service thanking God for his mercy and bounty. Friar Juan de Padilla promptly performed a Thanksgiving Mass, which was witnessed by a few baffled Teyas Indians.

We know too that Coronado and his men suffered travails aplenty in their quest for Quivira, the richest of the Seven Cities of Cibola, and that Coronado enlisted the aid of an Indian prisoner whom the Spanish called La Turque ("The Turk") because "he looked like one."

La Turque took the 1,500 men along with scores of horses, cattle and sheep on a hellish, meandering tour of the Llano Estacado, a vast expanse of shortgrass prairie with no settlements, no trees, very little water and nowhere to fix a compass. Coronado and his men wandered in dazed circles for days on end, lost, hungry and thirsty on an endless sea of grass. In this most desperate of states they made a final, harrowing descent into the Palo Duro.

A hailstorm hit the canyon the first night and stampeded the expedition's horses and destroyed much of their equipment. Hunters ventured onto the plains to kill buffalo, but the hunters got lost. Helpful comrades built fires and blew trumpets to help them find their way back to the canyon. Most of them eventually returned.

To this story many historians add a touch of balderdash. They point out that grapes and pecans, said to be a part of the feast, did not grow in the Palo Duro at that time. "There is now some doubt whether this was a special thanksgiving or a celebration of the Feast of the Ascension. It was held in Texas, but may have been on one of the forks of the Brazos River farther south," wrote Mike Kingston in an article written for the 1990–91 edition of the *Texas Almanac*.

The Thanksgiving story of the Rio Grande River as the site of the first feast centers on Juan de Onate, an aristocrat turned explorer who set out to explore territories that he had been granted north of the Rio Grande. In 1597, he bypassed a traditional route to blaze his own trail across the Chihuahuan Desert.

The trek did not go well.

First, there was the endless rain, which they prayed would stop. When it did, Onate, five hundred people and several hundred head of livestock nearly died of thirst. They went the last five days of the fifty-day journey with no food and no water. The expedition's arrival at the Rio Grande was its salvation.

After recuperating for ten days, Onate ordered a day of Thanksgiving. The feast consisted, we are told, of game hunted by the Spaniards and fish supplied by the natives of the region. The Franciscan missionaries traveling with the expedition performed a Mass. And finally, Onate read *La Toma*—"The Taking"—declaring the land drained by the Great River to be the possession of King Philip II of Spain.

A member of the expedition wrote of the original celebration, "We built a great bonfire and roasted the meat and fish, and then all sat down to a repast the like of which we had never enjoyed before."

Some historians call this one of the truly important dates in the history of the continent, marking the beginning of Spanish colonization in the American Southwest.

Others call it America's first Thanksgiving.

THE REINDEER OF TEXAS

Not a lot of people remember this, but there was a time when reindeer roamed wild in Texas and spread cheer and wonder all over the state and into several states beyond as well.

Okay, so the reindeer weren't wild. But they were here, all right, thanks almost entirely to the efforts of a man named Grady Carothers, a traditional Texas rancher who one day decided that he wanted to see reindeer in Texas.

Carothers's inspiration was his son who, being a native Texan, thought it mighty peculiar that Texas didn't have reindeer like some of those places "up north." Grady Carothers got to thinking about it and decided that other Texas children might like to see reindeer, too.

There was a time when reindeer could be found in Texas, especially around Christmas. *Library of Congress.*

Bringing reindeer to Texas is one of those things—like saving money or starting an exercise program—that is easier said than done. Carothers set about getting Texas its own reindeer, despite the guffaws of neighbors and otherwise good friends. He wrote a slew of letters to postmasters and various chambers of commerce in Alaska without so much as a reply from the Great White North.

Encouragement came from an unlikely source. The manager of a local department store told him that the Alaska Native Service managed reindeer for the Eskimo and that his best bet would be to get in touch with the service. Three times he was told "No," but Carothers was nothing if not persistent; he might even be called ornery and stubborn. Finally, Carothers was allowed to buy six reindeer steers despite the fact that the animals had never been that far south during a brutally hot August in Texas.

After getting the required permit in the summer of 1946, Carothers and his older son left the next day for Nome, Alaska. From there they traveled another one hundred miles east to Galvin, where Carothers bought six reindeer for fifty dollars apiece from an Eskimo.

The original Alaska reindeer were interlopers from Norway. They had been taken to Alaska from that country in 1891 to provide food and clothing for the Eskimos. One of the old Norwegians, who was wise in the ways of reindeer, persuaded Carothers to leave the reindeer with him in Seattle until fall, which Carothers did.

The Norwegian helped Grady break the reindeer, but there was a problem. The Norwegians and Alaskans had trained the reindeer to pull a sled. Carothers wanted them to drive a line. He eventually figured it out and in the process learned that reindeer can be as ornery and stubborn as any Texan.

Then there was the matter of feeding the critters. Texas was woefully short on reindeer moss—there wasn't any at all—but there wasn't a lot of the stuff in Alaska either. Carothers taught the reindeer, or they learned on their own, how to like cultivated food. But Carothers got some of the moss, when he could find it, and brought it back to Texas as a treat for the reindeer, which appropriately, if unoriginally, were named Dancer, Prancer, Donner and Vixen and the like.

These naturalized Texas reindeer wore red harnesses with their names stitched on them and pulled Santa in his sleigh from Thanksgiving through Christmas for more than forty years. Carothers contracted with local chambers of commerce, shopping centers and schools, putting on three shows per day and transporting the equipment in vans from town to town and state to state. It took three men, including Santa, to handle the reindeer.

Early on, the reindeer performed close to Carothers's ranch in Mills County, but their popularity extended all over the state and into thirty-nine southwestern and central states. Sometimes as many as six teams of reindeer were on the road at one time. One of the highlights came when he and his reindeer pulled Santa in a rose-covered sleigh in the 1955 Tournament of Roses Parade.

In time, Rudolph, a fawn with a red nose, joined the team and learned to travel in front of the harnessed deer. Rudolph had his own harness with his name and little bells. He was quite the prima donna.

Carothers ended up making fifteen more trips to Alaska to get more reindeer, including some females so that he could have his own replacements, ones that were native Texans to boot. He and his reindeer were profiled in several newspapers and magazines, including the January 1954 edition of *Wide World*.

The reindeer were kept on Carothers's ranch in Mills County until Carothers and Son Enterprises moved to California, where the animals were exhibited at Santa Claus Land and shown in fall parades. He sold the reindeer and equipment in 1984 and drove the stagecoach at Knott's Berry Farm.

"It wasn't easy, but nothing ever is," Carothers said of his reindeer operation.

Carothers died in April 25, 2004, one day after his ninety-eighth birthday in Gonzales County, California. He is buried at Senterfit Cemetery near Lometa. And the reindeer, like the buffalo and others before them, no longer roam in Texas.

BIBLIOGRAPHY

Bedichek, Roy. *Adventures of a Texas Naturalist*. Austin: University of Texas Press, 1947.

Caro, Robert. "Sad Irons." *Unknown Texas*. Edited by Jonathan Eisen and Harold Straughn. New York: Macmillan Publishing Co., 1988.

Cartwright, Walter J. "The Cedar Chopper." *Southwest Historical Quarterly* 70, no. 2 (October 1966).

Coleman, Loren. *Tom Slick and the Search for the Yeti*. London: Faber and Faber, 1989.

Couffer, Jack. *Bat Bomb: World War II's Other Secret Weapon*. Austin: University of Texas Press, 2008.

Cox, Mike. *Fred Gipson: Texas Storyteller*. Austin, TX: Shoal Creek Publishers, 1980.

Davis, Steven L. *J. Frank Dobie: A Liberated Mind*. Austin: University of Texas Press, 2009.

Debo, Darrell. *History of Burnet County*. 2 vols. Austin, TX: Eakin Press, 1960.

Eisenhour, Virginia. *Alex Sweet's Texas*. Austin: University of Texas Press, 1986.

Essin, Emmett M. *Shavetails and Bell Sharps: History of the U.S. Army Mule*. Lincoln: University of Nebraska Press, 2000.

Fowler, Gene. *Mavericks: A Gallery of Texas Characters*. Austin: University of Texas Press, 2008.

Frantz, Joe B. *Texas: A Bicentennial History*. New York: W.W. Norton and Company, Inc., 1976.

Gantwell, Robert. "The Cowboy Who Showed Them." *Sports Illustrated* (May 9, 1977).

Gillespie County Historical Society. *Pioneers in God's Hills*. 2 vols. Austin, TX: Von-Boeckmann-Jones, 1960.

Gipson, Fred. *An Acceptance Speech*. New York: Harper, 1960.

———. *Old Yeller*. New York: Harper, 1956.

Greene, A.C. *The 50+ Best Books on Texas*. Denton: University of North Texas Press, 1998.

———. *Sketches from the Five States of Texas*. College Station: Texas A&M University Press, 1998.

Handbook of Texas online. www.handbookoftexas. Various entries.

Hunter, J. Marvin. *Lyman Wight Colony in Texas*. Bandera, TX: Frontier Times Museum, 1952.

Johnson, David. *The Mason County "Hoo Doo" War, 1874–1902*. Denton: University of North Texas Press, 2009.

Kansas City Journal. "Texas Gold Finds." February 7, 1898. Accessed online.

Moursund, John. *Blanco County History*. Burnet, TX: Nortex, 1979.

New York Times. "Fortunes Sunk In Mines." March 20, 1898. Accessed online.

Porter, William Sydney. *O. Henry's Texas Stories*. Dallas, TX: Still Point Press, 1986.

Quammen, David. *Natural Acts*. New York: Dell Publishing, 1985.

Shrake, Bud. "Having Themselves a Blast." *Sports Illustrated* (July 16, 1973).

———. "The Once Forbidding Land." *Land of the Permanent Wave*. Edited by Steven L. Davis. Austin: University of Texas Press, 2008.

Sitton, Thad. *Harder Than Hardscrabble*. Austin: University of Texas Press, 2003.

Smith, C. Alphonso. *O. Henry Biography*. Whitefish, MT: Kessinger Publisher, n.d.

Smithwick, Noah. *Evolution of a State*. Austin, TX: Gammel, 1900. Reprint Austin: University of Texas Press, 2003.

Toepperwein, Fritz. *Charcoal and Charcoal Burners*. Boerne, TX: Highland Press, 1950.

Whisenhunt, Donald W. *Texas: A Sesquicentennial Celebration*. Austin, TX: Eakin Press, 1985.

Wilbarger, J.W. *Indian Depredations in Texas*. Austin, TX: Eakin Press, 1991.

Woolley, Bryan. "The Dying Birthplace of Texas." *The Edge of the West and Other Texas Stories*. El Paso: Texas Western Press, 1992.

Zelade, Richard. *Hill Country*. Austin, TX: Gulf Publishing Company, 1999.

INDEX

ABOUT THE AUTHOR

Clay Coppedge is a journalist and freelance writer who grew up in Lubbock, Texas, and has lived and worked as a sportswriter and regional reporter for several central Texas newspapers over the last four decades. His work has appeared in a wide range of publications, including *Acres USA*, the *Austin Chronicle*, *Field & Stream*, *Texas Co-op Power*, *Texas Golfer*, *Texas Highways* and others.

Visit us at
www.historypress.net